Short Shrift

A Memoir of John Robertson Innes 1917 to 1958

By John Innes copyright 15/1/ 2024

E-Mail, innespahill@yahoo.co.uk

Especially for his daughter Pam, his boys Ross and Robert and their respective partners Angie and Joyce, and all other descendants of John Robertson Innes

		Page No
	Introduction	5
Chapter 1	Earliest Memories	6
Chapter 2	Scotland the Brave	10
Chapter 3	Boyhood and RAF	14
Chapter 4	Happy Days	19
Chapter 5	Recreation	24
Chapter 6	At His Best	28
Chapter 7	At the Flicks	36
Chapter 8	Critical Times	39
Chapter 9	Great Changes	43
Chapter 10	Holidays and Health	48
Chapter 11	Material Growth	54
Chapter 12	Heartbreak and Generosity	61
Chapter 13	Too Little Too Late	65
Chapter 14	Farewell to Scotland	71
Chapter 15	Final Fling	86

		Page No
Chapter 16	Compassion	96
Chapter 17	Nostalgia	99
Chapter 18	A Bitter Blow	103
	Conclusion	109

Introduction

John Roberson Innes was born on the 26th ^{of} January 1917 to Robert Whyte Innes and Isabella Innes, nee McCuaig.

He was born in Glasgow where he lived until he joined the R.A.F. at the age of twenty in 1937.
He married Marjorie Ruth Underhill in 1944, in the town of Smethwick.

Was honourably discharged from the Airforce in 1949.
After his marriage, he lived mainly in Smethwick and Quinton in the Midland's area, until he died in 1958 at the age of forty-one.
This is my perspective on him and is purely my view and opinion drawn from living with him for twelve years. I have tried to be as objective as possible but considering my position as his son it's probably impossible.

Human memory is fallible and mine is, "no objection to the rule" Throughout, I have tried my best to give an accurate account of events and to keep some sort of chronological order. Time is of the essence and my success at finding any additional material grows more improbable over time.

Records and photographs are scant and have been scattered in many directions and I wanted to put this on record for his remaining children and their descendants.

John Innes Gloucester 2023

Chapter1 Earliest Memories

It was a bright sunny day, and my attention was drawn by a commotion, caused by the arrival of a stranger and all the excitement surrounding him. I was transfixed, on tiptoes, staring over the large table, that dominated the living room. Only those familiar with the family would have come that way, he had arrived unannounced, suddenly, appearing in the corner between the sideboard and the radio. He must have come through by the backdoor, entering the living room from the kitchen.

The stranger was very smartly dressed, wearing unusual blue clothes, on his head perched at a cheeky angle was a forage cap decorated with sparkling gold insignia. A broad smile of pleasure and delight illuminated his face, over his shoulder he'd slung a huge kit bag. We all rushed to surround him, Mom, Grandma, big sister Sonya, and little three-year-old me, for the merest of moments there was an awkward silence. Then the stranger spoke "Look what I've brought for you" he said in a strange but somehow familiar accent. He immediately swung the huge bag onto the table causing Gran to call out in a concerned voice, "John be careful!" releasing the drawstrings he pulled out a great muslin cloth, it was protecting a precious gift about the size of a shoebox. He unwrapped it by holding one end of the cloth and gently rolling its contents out. Its golden treasure oozing a sweet syrupy liquid, I shouted incredulously "What is it?" Mom answered excitedly "That's a honeycomb". Sonya and I squealed with surprise and anticipation; sweets had just been put back on ration after a short reprieve at the end of April, and the long shadow of the Second World War was still detrimentally affecting the UK, long after the conflict had ended.

It was my dad! and he had finally come home never to leave us again. This was my very earliest memory of him, he was here! In the living room of Grandma's house, in Smethwick, it was difficult to take it all in. The date was most probably August of 1949, the date of his final discharge from the Royal Air Force.

His home for the foreseeable future would be a small two-storied terraced house built in the early 1900s. It consisted of; on the first floor three bedrooms, on the ground floor a front room rarely used, and the living room with a black lead fireplace. This is where all the cooking was done and the main area of family activity. Finally, through to the back - kitchen with an earthenware sink, one cold water tap, and a coal-heated boiler used on washing day, traditionally always on a Monday. It was built of brick supporting a large cast iron cauldron, covered by a huge wooden lid. Exiting by the back door, via the kitchen you would pass "The Mangle" a monstrous cast-iron contraption, used to squeeze out most of the water from the washing. If you were looking for relief, you would find it outside, in a corrugated roofed lean-to, abutting the kitchen. It had a sloping roof and was divided into three, a coal shed, W.C., and finally a small shed for garden tools. In the wall next to the coal shed was inserted a heavy iron hook from which hung a large tin bath used every week on "bath night". Its second function was securing one end of the clothesline.

Late at night, Mom occasionally used the corrugated roof to gain access to the house. It had a slope that, with a little effort, would allow you to climb to the windowsill of the small bedroom located at the back of the house. The lowest point of the roof being only about four feet from the ground, she could clamber onto this with the aid of the Dustbin, and grunting, groaning, and shushing, drag herself and us kids to the window, and climb in. When asked why we needed to enter by this precarious route, she would say she had forgotten the keys and didn't want to disturb Gran. It could have been we'd been locked out after some argument. Dad was never involved in these events so he may have been out, or away at the time.

Dad had come home to his immediate family but because of housing shortages after the war, he had to live in the home of his wife's parents. They were kindly warm loving people, so although the circumstances were difficult, they welcomed their Scottish, ex-RAF son-in-law into their home.

Both Mom and Dad met while they were both serving in the RAF and after becoming pregnant in late 1943, Mom had to apply for compassionate leave. Forcing her to move back to live with her parents. This would also be about the time she married Dad in early 1944. She gave birth to Sonya in August of that year and Dad would have visited her from time to time, when granted leave. What his activities were, and how much time he was allowed between the RAF, and his family is not clear from his official records.

We lived with Gran's until the 6th of April 1954, these were the best years I can remember for our little family. However, within those ten years, he did try to assert his independence and find a new life for us in Glasgow. How he managed to persuade Mom, to experiment with this relocation, is difficult to imagine. Her youth may have given her a more optimistic view of the situation. The full details have unfortunately been lost over time, sadly it proved a short-lived venture and a failure.

Chapter 2 Scotland the Brave

It was possibly the constraints of living with his wife's parents and getting a new start after the hardships of serving in the forces during wartime, that motivated him to return to Glasgow. It was during our very early days in Smethwick, possibly early 1946 to early 1948, that this futile attempt was made. Exactly when this was and for how long remains a mystery to me. I did on several occasions try to find out more by asking Mom, but disconcertingly her benign facial expression would change immediately, to one of anger mixed with frustration. Shaking her head and hands in unison she would say "I can't remember." Realising, I was pursuing an area far too painful for her to recall. Also, causing her great displeasure, so I would swiftly change the subject.

Over the years, a few memories of her time in Glasgow slipped out, but always talking with a third party, with me overhearing; the story of my ear problems, when she took me to the Hospital. Laughing with a friend over "the awful cake" our Scottish Grandad made for some family event, the irony of which, he was a baker by profession. The wonderful Italian ice creams available in Glasgow, which had a large Italian immigrant population at that time dominating the ice cream market. The "ice cream" wars are legendary in Glasgow mythology and are still talked about today. Why we went and the reason for returning to Smethwick I can only surmise. Dad may have wanted us to be with his family in Glasgow and get away from the influences surrounding Mom's life and her family.

She possibly became unhappy there, living in an alien environment, away from her family and friends, further exacerbated by Sonya being moved to London and our health problems. Sonya was the eldest child, our big sister, she went for a short time, to live with Mom's sister Aunt Lillian in London. This was to recover her health and possibly towards the end of our stay in Glasgow.

We lived in Glasgow for a relatively short period, probably about two years in total. Possibly living with Dad's older brother Robert and his wife Doris, in tenement-block, at number 5 Portman Street, Glasgow in about the years 1946/48. This is today, the site of commercial units the tenements have long gone. It may have given Mom's parents some temporary relief, but we soon returned to Smethwick.

Dad's Mom, Isabella (Sonya's middle name) passed away in 1947, so we were possibly there during this sad event. It was said that she died of a heart attack while getting into a hot bath. It makes me happy that she may have held me in her arms before her passing, but sadly I have no memories of her.

However, several abiding memories from our time there, still exist in my aging brain. How accurate these are is for the reader to decide. At what age we can store memories and keep them for future recall is one of those mysteries, argued over by so-called experts and I was very young. Also, memory of an event can vary considerably between witnesses as any police officer will tell you. Having no hard facts to go on, I can only guess that I was possibly under twelve months old when we arrived in Glasgow, and under three when we returned to Smethwick.

My earliest memory is going into a room with people dressed all in green with face masks, everywhere painted cream and green. Swinging doors with circular windows and being terrified as a fine net contraption was placed over my face. Learning, many years later, that I'd had caught a severe ear infection and had a very high temperature. Mom carried me one freezing night, through a snowstorm to a local hospital, where I was operated on, and this was possibly my memory of this event.

In recent years, I was watching an old T.V. documentary involving medical operations on small children. It was then the "penny dropped;" they were using a net contraption like a gauze mask onto which a combination of, Ether, Chloroform, and Oxygen was put, to anesthetise them. Placing it over a child's face, drops were gently poured onto the net. They evaporated, and the gas produced, was breathed in by the child, causing unconsciousness. This must have been the very instrument they put over my face and used in my operation. The aftermath of this resulted in my severe aversion to anything made of net, curtains made of net caused a particularly bad reaction, shaking with fear when near to them. This subsided as I grew older, but a residue of fear remains, the reason for this aversion not being understood for many years.

Other memories of living in Glasgow's Tenements, are still retained by me. Running in the backyard with my sister, playing in the snow, laughing and throwing snowballs at each other, Mom, keeping "an eye on us" in the washhouse doing the laundry. Running in and watching her kneading the clothes in the hot water with suds flying about in all directions. Dashing over to the open window of the kitchen to see Dad's sister-in-law Doris, who was merrily preparing the vegetables for dinner. She was singing and laughing, poking raw carrots through a metal grid for us to nibble on.

Packing up to leave Glasgow and return to Smethwick was my last memory of this short period. My parents made me leave my most treasured possession, a red tin crane. It broke my heart, and its sad loss has never been reconciled. In recent years, I found a much beaten-up one in an antique shop and purchased it for display in my living room. Later, I saw one in a posh antique shop in the Cotswolds, it was almost in perfect condition, but its price was unfortunately way beyond my limited income, so I had to pass on it.

The return train journey to Smethwick has only one lasting memory. Lying on my back in the railway carriage, trying to sleep, looking up and seeing countless telephone poles pass by and observing the multitude of wires festooned from their tops like twelve-stringed guitars. Today, you would need to look at old photographs on the days of steam to fully experience their evocative charm.

You may well ask where Dad was, in this period, I can only surmise he must have been around, at least some of the time. Looking at his RAF records he was given partial release in 1946 but remained on reserve until his discharge on the 11th of July 1949. So exactly what his RAF duties were during those three years and how much time he spent away or at home with us, his family, will be probably impossible to find out.

Chapter 3 Boyhood and RAF

He joined the RAF on the 10th of March 1937 and was discharged on the 11th of July 1949, serving for just over twelve years, including the war years. On his records, he is said to be of very good character. His rank for the first two years was AC2(aircraft hand), then for a period in 1940, his rank became LAC (leading aircraftman), and his trade classification clerk/teleprinter operator. This role lasted till 1941, he was then promoted to corporal, a rank he retained for the rest of his time in the service. At the beginning of 1941, he became an Equipment Assistant which means he worked in the stores, all through his career in the RAF his work performance is recorded as satisfactory, whatever that means. It also states in his records, that he was promoted in 1939 to Leading Aircraftsman after examination in Doncaster, where he achieved a B classification. Also, in 1944 he gained a level of proficiency regarding petrol installations.

In 1946 his records show he was on some sort of release, that's possibly the period when he took us to try and settle in Scotland and our return possibly in 1948, he was fully discharged in 1949.

His locations varied during his time in the RAF and do not always line up with his official records, the following is what the official documents say, later I will explain other locations not listed.

In the official records, we start at Uxbridge, London. Then for a short period in Chigwell: a few miles northeast of London, before being posted in 1938 to Doncaster with the 616 squadron. He was stationed here till being posted in 1940 to Sullom Voe, in the Shetland Islands north of Scotland. This posting lasted nearly two years, till the end of 1941 when he was posted to Swailwell it clearly stated twice on his record, but I can find no such place. The nearest to that spelling is RAF Snailwell near Newmarket in Cambridgeshire, he was there for nearly two years. Then in 1943, he was sent to units in Redcar in the northeast of England, where he spent about 18 months before being finally posted to Mildenhall, Wiltshire in February 1946.

In the later part of 1943, he must have been in Birdlip near Gloucester, although from his postings you would think he was in Redcar some two hundred and forty miles away. We know this because Mom conceived Sonya in Birdlip in November of that year. They often talked about it, Sonya pointing out a phone box at the bottom of Birdlip Hill, opposite the Twelve Bells pub. The phone box is sadly no longer there, taken away with the advent of the mobile phone. Sonya would jokingly say "I bet that's where I was conceived" Incidentally, family legend has it being the pub where Mom and Dad had their first date.

Mom was also stationed at Birdlip during the war, so in the 1990's she went on a nostalgic trip with Sonya, and I believe brother Robert also accompanied them, to find where she had been billeted. A site halfway down Birdlip Hill, she said, "I used to look out of the Nissen hut window and see him run by in his shorts and really fancy him" Today, there is little evidence left of their occupation, the ground had long been cleared and reclaimed by nature. However, the large Radar masts and the surrounding buildings on top of Birdlip Hill can still be seen.

Also, I can remember Dad telling me that he spent time in France but there is no record of it, maybe the RAF kept their official postings fixed but seconded personnel on a more flexible basis, unrecorded.

He gave me some salt-stained German pilot badges, one I remember distinctly, a flying eagle with the swastika gripped in its talons. He told me he'd cut them from dead German pilot's uniforms who had crashed in the sea after they'd been shot down in the first wave of attacks on England. One story he told me, with a wry smile on his face, shocked me at the time but I was very young. He told me that when recruits arrived, they carried out a billet initiation ceremony. It consisted of debagging them, (taking off their trousers) and smearing their private parts with black boot polish. Also, they engaged in brewing illicit alcohol in their free time, I can imagine being in places like Sullom Voe you would need some distractions. This would have been a tough assignment, long hours of monotony it's possible he learned to row a boat there, being surrounded by the sea.

His RAF records list his height as being, five feet seven and a half inches, hair colour dark brown, eyes brown his complexion as fresh, he had a vaccination scar on his left arm, scars on his back, and an appendix scar. I remember him telling me when he was a young boy, he was out playing with his friends when he was suddenly struck with tremendous stomach pain and had to be rushed to hospital. Luckily, they removed his appendix and saved his life.

Many people from his generation had a very noticeable, round vaccination scar, on their arm, I think Mother had one too, it was to prevent smallpox which was eradicated a long time ago. He also had a series of round scars on his back, Sonya and I noticed them when he fell off a step ladder. He was putting up a pelmet in the living room, he slipped and fell heavily from the ladders onto his face. The fall tore his shirt, revealing his bare back, we both gasped with horror at the sight of several, large round scars on his back. The fact that they are reported on his RAF records means they must have been inflicted before he was twenty years old. We never asked, and he never told us how he received them. He also had a noticeable scar on his temple, in this instance, I did ask him how it happened. He told me a filing cabinet fell on him when he was in the RAF.

Dad rarely reminisced about his boyhood. One day I was reading a magazine with an iconic photograph of young black boys in the USA, laughing and eating watermelons, fruit I'd never seen. Rationing was still restricting the range of foods available to us in the UK and melons were very much a luxury and rarely seen in the 1950's. "What's this" I asked showing it to Dad, and with a smile on his face he told me back in Glasgow when he was a boy, he often used to buy slices of watermelons on hot summer days.

He also told me, he was out one night with his mates, when they got into a fracas with some youths, carrying knives. Smiling, he told me they disarmed them and used their knives to cut off their ties.

Chapter 4 Happy Days

So, by 1949 we were all together back in Smethwick, Mom, Dad, my sister Sonya, and me living with Grandma. Sadly, my grandfather passed away in April, from lung cancer. We must have returned from Glasgow by then because I can remember being chastised for climbing on the doctor's car and bending back the windscreen wipers. Also, asking why all the curtains in the neighbourhood were drawn, in those days people did it as a mark of respect on the day of a funeral. The one positive effect of the loss of grandad was mom quit smoking and never relapsed. She blamed Woodbine cigarettes for Grandad's demise, one of the cheapest brands on the market (coffin nails in the vernacular) She was with him at the very end of his life, seeing him coughing up the contents of his lungs and choking. This had a saltatory effect on her and to her credit, she never took up the habit again. Later in life she repeatedly asked Sonya to pack up smoking, she was unfortunately a very heavy smoker. To avoid the issue, she even told Mom she'd stopped, going as far as not lighting up in Mom's presence. This deception only lasted a short time and she soon returned to her old habit, unable to quit or deceive mum.

Dad had been finally released from the RAF, so he had to find a job, from comments made by Mom, he worked as a Glass sorter. This must have been for a very short period; it could have been at Chance's Glass Works in Smethwick, which was one of the largest employers in the area, now sadly long gone. Many years ago, I remember reading a job reference letter, from a long-forgotten electrical company, extolling his attributes as a valued employee.

This may have been to support his application to join B.T.H., (British Thomas and Houston) who later became A.E.I. a large manufacturer of electrical components, a long-forgotten company absorbed and dismantled by the asset stripers, that have long plagued this country. They had a considerable electric motor manufacturing facility just a few miles away in Blackheath, West Midlands. He would have joined them in the very early 1950`s possibly in the buying office. This is purely conjecture on my part, and based on his next and final job, in which I know for certain, he was employed as a buyer. By a strange coincidence, I too became a buyer and by the late 1970`s a corporate member of the Institute of Purchasing and Supply, now called the Chartered Institute of Procurement and Supply. This was not by design but just by a series of fortunate opportunities. My mention of this may seem to the reader boastful and lacking in modesty, but it's really to advise, that for many years I felt Dad was always there with me, in the spiritual sense, supporting and guiding me.

It was during his time that he took up Archery, B.T.H. his employer, had invested in an extensive sports facility for its workers and staff. It was very close to the factory and surrounded by very tall Poplar trees. Dad took me there a few times to watch him fire his arrows into large round, coloured targets. This also helps me date this period, I can clearly remember Dad`s quiver full of arrows hanging from a hook, on Grandma's living room wall, just below the clock. So, he must have been working there when we lived in Smethwick with Grandma, and also after we moved to our new house in Quinton, which I will talk about later. This is because between the sports ground and our new home was Brandhall Golf

Course, my friends and I often played around its periphery. Here, I would always wave to Dad as he walked by, but I never remember him responding, just looking slightly embarrassed and indifferent, concentrating on returning home after a day at the office. It was quite a pleasant walk for him, particularly in good weather. This meant that he was still working for B.T.H. after 6th April 1954 but this could only have been for a short time; because he was with his final employer Philips Cycles for several years and was employed by them when he passed- away. Several of his work colleagues attended the funeral, and they made a welcome contribution towards its expenses.

Some years later, in the latter half of 1965, the beginning of 1966, I took an engineering course at Dad`s old company B.T.H. By then it had changed its name to A.E.I. and it was possibly ten years since Dad had worked there. One day I was approached by a man and a woman, a couple of office workers, to tell me they remembered him, all I can recall of this encounter was, that they said, "he was a very nice man". The reason I can quite accurately date this is because Sonny and Cher`s "I've Got You Babe" was a big hit at the time and playing at a nearby pub. Incidentally, the first-ever jet engine, invented by Sir Frank Whittle was developed under the auspices of B.T.H.

When we lived in White Road Smethwick, I would often wait for Dad on the corner of the road, hoping to see him on his way back from work. This would be between five and six in the evening, and I would be around five years old. Excitedly, I would run up to him, and he would occasionally have a small gift for me. Once he had several marble-sized silver shiny balls, much later I realized they were ball bearings, used extensively in the production of electric motors, but at the time were a much-prized gift.

On another occasion he brought me a silver pocket watch, I wore it proudly, particularly at school, but it took a few years to pass before I could tell the time. Unfortunately, by then the watch had sadly disintegrated. The most memorable event in this episode still leaves me with shame and regret. One hot summer evening, running up to him as usual, he said "Here's sixpence go and get you and Sonya an ice cream" Greedily, I scoffed mine on the way home, but temptation soon overwhelmed me, and I couldn't resist eating my sisters too. Happily thinking I had got away with it, both fooling my dad; and getting one over on my troublesome sister. Later, during the evening meal, Dad asked my sister "Did you enjoy your ice cream?" she responded, "But I haven't had any ice cream" Retribution was swift and painful with a slap around the ear, his favourite method of punishment, dismissing me from the table. It must have dented his faith in me at the time and possibly, justifiably thereafter, for I can never remember him asking me to buy ice cream, on behalf of anyone again. My weakness and moral dilemma with ice cream remains part of my psyche to this very day.

How long Sonya stayed with Auntie Lilian in London is not on record, but an affinity for her aunt stayed with her for the rest of her life. Every year, in the summer she would be invited back for a short holiday, so I think the affection was reciprocated. I must have found it cold and lonely, sleeping in the little back bedroom at Grans, without her. So, in the middle of the night, I used to run into the larger middle bedroom where Mum and Dad were fast asleep and cuddled down between them.

The feeling of warmth, comfort, and security was overwhelmingly wonderful. I can`t imagine in the whole realm of human experience, a more perfect way of achieving Shangri-La. Suddenly, just as I thought I'd achieved the ultimate state of "being" the cold hard voice, I always dreaded, would break the silence of the night. Mom would shout "John! get him back into his own bed" Dad wakened by this, would drag himself out of bed, barely conscious. Pick me up, and in a confused foggy state of annoyance carry me back, to a cold and lonely bed.

Inquisitive kids can be a nightmare and Sonya and I were no exception, crawling under Mom and Dad's bed one day, Sonya and I found an unusual bottle. When we examined its contents, we found it contained very large, waxy, cream-coloured tablets, we didn't know what they were but guessed from the location it might be something naughty. We giggled and put them back, never daring to ask what they were for. Many years later, I realised that they were spermicide tablets a very ineffective method of contraception. Which turned out to be lucky for me and my other siblings.

Chapter 5 Recreation- West Smethwick Park

Smoking was an important part of Dad's life and at weekends he would have a lie-in, puffing away on a cigarette, reading a book or paper in bed, grandma, Mom, and Sonya would be up and about, so I would sidle up to him for a cuddle and he would laugh and joke with me. Showing me the packet of cigarettes and letting me play with them, I would be about three years old. In these very early days, two of his favourite brands were Turf and Guards, I was intrigued by the artwork on them. Turf cigarettes were blue and silver, using Pegasus as the logo and Guards were mainly pale green with the picture of a guardsman proudly displayed on the front. Somewhere, I must have seen a boy using wings attached to his ankles to give him the power of flight. So, I would cut out the silver wings, which were printed large on the cigarette packet, and attach them to my shoes. Imagining I had the power of flight, like the boys in a comic or a Rupert the Bear story, I was an avid consumer of both.

He also flirted from time to time with pipe smoking although it never became a constant habit. At Grans, he had some long stemmed very old-style clay pipes called `Churchwardens` and much later the traditional brier pipe. Once, without his knowledge, I borrowed his brier pipe together with a tin of his preferred tobacco "Gold Block," and smoked it at a nearby pub car park with some friends. Soon I began to feel sick and giddy and sneaked it back to him never in my youth to try it again. Whether or not he found out I don`t remember, possibly I got away with it, I`m sure my memory would have recalled such an event, particularly if a painful punishment was metered out.

Soaking in a glass on the bedside table would be his false teeth, where or when he lost his own remains a mystery. It was common practice, particularly amongst the working classes, to have them all removed. This avoided costly dentistry and future painful episodes of toothache. Gum disease may also have been a contributory factor, without modern medicine such as antibiotics, it may have been the only treatment for painful abscesses.

Smethwick was a typical industrial town and had some lovely parks to brighten up the grim lives of its inhabitants, but nothing could compare with the real countryside. To alleviate our frustration Dad decided to take Sonya and me to the Lickey Hills for a day's outing. They still ran trams up to that famous Brummie beauty spot, Mom didn't come with us. It was a sublime day, I was only about five and Sonya six, we had a fantastic time. My strongest memories are being intrigued by the massive tree roots growing everywhere, along the paths and roads, and the freedom of running about in the woods and being happy.

Dad would have been in his early thirties when we lived with grandma in Smethwick, he seemed very fit and healthy in those early days. Work would have taken up much of his time, but on Sundays, he would take me, and often Sonya to West Smethwick Park for a few hours' recreation. The boat ride on the lake was one of our favourites, he took an excellent photograph of us sitting in a rowing boat. Sonya gave a copy to the Smethwick Heritage Centre, which they reproduced for the month of March in their 2019 calendar, sadly she passed away in July of that year.

Just a few days after her passing, I was sitting waiting for a tyre change in a local garage. In walked a bright young man in his early thirties, with dark thick wavy hair, and a fresh complexion, he was about my height, well-proportioned, and physically fit. We started chatting and he gave me a feeling of happiness and positivity towards life, unfortunately, the details of our conversation I cannot recall. He had a Scottish accent and I asked what he did for a living, he said he was a radar operator in the R.A.F. At the time, I thought no more but as the days passed, I wondered if it was Dad's presence, reassuring me after the loss of Sonya. This is not an imaginary event, made up to spice up my account of Dad's life, but a true real-life experience, and I find it difficult to encompass it, in my belief system. However, the aftermath leaves me feeling that it was my dad and it's how I would have expected him to have been, in the prime of his life.

One of the main highlights of our visits to the park was taking refreshments at the café. It was a large circular building constructed mainly of wood and glass painted green, located right in the middle you could easily have mistaken it for an arboretum. Here we would have a cup of tea and a rock cake, its only drawback being the massive, and austere Victorian portraits of the Chance family, looking down from their high position near the ceiling. They were the owners of a large and prestigious glass company in Smethwick, donating funds for the people of the town to enjoy the recreational facilities of a park. Dad also taught me how to play crown green bowling on the park's bowling green, now sadly gone to seed. I can see him now, casting forward the round rubber mat onto the beautifully kept green lawn.

Rotating between his hands a huge black, heavy, highly polished bowel, feeling for its weight, stepping forward, holding it in his right hand. Then, with a swift pendulum-like forward motion, dropping his knee onto the rubber mat, releasing the bowel so it could roll gently towards the smaller white Jack. After, we would stroll around to the "Sons of Rest" to enjoy its peace and tranquillity; I believe it was for the veterans of the Great War. It had lovely cream-painted cabins surrounding a beautifully kept garden of remembrance, and we would sit there and enjoy the peace of the moment. In later years, when reminiscing about the lovely times spent in the park with Dad, Mom would say; she had to nag him to get him to do anything with us. Maybe, it's true but I would like to think he gained some pleasure from it.

Chapter 6 At His Best

Memory is often fragmented, almost like photographs in an album. Stitching them together in a consistent and flowing way presents its difficulties. The following are some of these snapshot memories gathered while still living with Grandma.

Dad was in the kitchen, kneeling down constructing a framework to support Grandma's earthenware sink. Mum, was taking us out, passing him in a rather tight spot, going out for some long-forgotten reason. His dark brown eyes met with mine, just for a second, he gave me a warm loving smile as we said goodbye. The moment might not have registered, but unusually he was at my eye level and not towering above me. Also, he didn't smile or seem happy very often, he mostly appeared to me sad, serious, and sometimes angry. One very hot day, I was surprised by Dad rushing into the kitchen, hot and sweating grabbing a pint of milk and drinking the whole bottle all in one go. It amazed me at the time, but I have on occasion done the same myself and always recall that powerful and impressive moment.

A very special treat for me was a visit to the very auspicious Harry Mitchell cricket ground in Smethwick. What Dad's motive was I can only guess; the availability of drink! but I enjoyed the visits, sitting on the grass on a warm summer's day watching the cricket with my Dad. Not realising, that the game was anathema to most Scotsmen, he may have been the exception, but I doubt it!

In the years between 1949 and 1954 my sister and I went to Devonshire Road school, incidentally, it was Mom's junior school too. One day, there was great excitement when they obtained their first film projector, and subsequently, we began to be shown educational films, and feature films, on special occasions. It was a complete surprise; when I was told by one of the teachers my dad had supplied it. The company he worked for B.T.H. did make film projectors, how he managed to obtain one, I never found out and he never mentioned it to me.

An endearing episode occurred in 1951; a severe flu epidemic was sweeping the country. Mum and Gran were laid up, so it was left to Dad to care for everybody, he did this quietly and calmly. Cooking and cleaning and keeping us kids entertained. The food as I remember was mainly mashed potato, nevertheless, it was extremely filling. It was during this period that he tried to do some "Home Education" by purchasing a children's educational book. The cover was a semi-rigid canvas-type material, with a cream-coloured background, printed black and red. The front was decorated with a drawing of a boy and a girl. This optimistic attempt, however, did not last long, trying to educate two unruly kids must have been soul-destroying for him.

He was an avid reader, and one of his preferences was American crime novels, he took me on my first visit to a library a very grand building on the High Street, and I was very impressed. It started off my habit of joining the local library wherever I lived, a gift that provided many years of education, pleasure, and enjoyment.

One day that year, I was idly looking out of gran's back window when I observed two strange women entering the back gate. The taller one had heavily permed, light brown hair, both were very slim and carrying suitcases. They both spoke with the same accent as Dad, I found the situation very amusing. They were his relatives, possibly his beloved sisters-in-law, Doris and May. They stayed for a few days, how Grandma fitted them in, I can't imagine but she was always very accommodating. Mom searched the contents of their suitcases and laughed and joked about how poor their clothes were. But what amused her most, were bottles of gin and the condoms she found.

It was over a book, that I once infuriated him so much he struck me. He instructed me to go upstairs and look for it by his bedside. I searched high and low but failed to find it. On my return to Gran's living room, where he was seated impatiently waiting. I reported back and told him I couldn't find it. He struck me and was extremely angry, shouting and swearing. Later, that day, smiling and laughing he said "Johnny, I've found that book, it wasn't upstairs after all, but the slap will do for next time."

He was proud of being Scottish, and one day he drew my attention to an incident he'd found extremely amusing, pointing out in his newspaper, that some Scottish students had stolen the "Stone of Scone". In the middle of the night, they went into Westminster Abbey and stole it, and then took it back to Scotland. It was the Christmas morning of 1950, and I can remember him showing me the pictures, smiling and laughing in triumph, exclaiming loudly; "well it was stolen by the English in the first place anyway."

Often, he would tell me how the Scots had beaten the English at Bannockburn, he pointed to the green fields where the battle had taken place when we visited Scotland, all those years ago. In very recent times, I visited this sacred ground and was dismayed to see a 1970s housing estate had been built on the site. Only the Scots would desecrate, arguably their most important and hallowed soil. The place where they gained freedom from English domination forever. Selling out for money, well it is possibly in their culture. He was also well-versed in all the Scottish contributions to the arts and sciences. This propaganda made me want to be Scottish, my sister had a Scottish trinket that I coveted, it was a piece of deer antler the size and shape of a 'Nice' biscuit with a tartan ribbon passing through two slots, and one side had a safety pin the other a gold-plated metal motif of a stag's head. It was fought over several times but who won the battle? I suppose my sister did.

Any delusions I had about being Scottish ended one day when in a fit of anger, his face turned purple and contorted with rage. He pointed down to my little face and with an accusing finger through his gritted teeth shouted, "Johnny you English have never beaten us, and you never will" Someone possibly with malice of forethought, had told me that the Scots were a bunch of Irish immigrants and parrot-like I had repeated to him, not realising the consequences. On another occasion I repeated a rude song somebody had taught me; I can still remember the words to this day which are too disgusting to repeat here. The consequences were severe and painful, at the time I had no idea what they meant and how depraved they were.

He liked a drink but in the early days it wasn't too excessive, when taking me out on trips, he would go into a pub en route, for a pint of beer. This was before we had a car, so we mainly walked or caught a bus. Public houses were not so child-friendly in those days. So, I had to wait outside. Sometimes, it would seem like hours, causing me great distress.

On Saturday mornings we would walk from Smethwick to West Bromwich. Crossing over Galton Bridge, passing the old coal mine workings with its ruined winding wheel, looking broken and forlorn, to a pub with a boxing club attached. Here we would work out and practice the art of Boxing and its associated exercise regime. It smelled of sweat mixed with embrocation cream. Men of all ages and types were busily carrying out their various fitness programs. Skipping, sparring, running on treadmills, bench pressing, weightlifting, etc. They were in all various stages of undress, some naked, others wearing jockstraps, some in leotards, it was all very bewildering and overwhelming to me.

Dad loved swimming, he said he came second in a major swimming competition in the RAF, beaten by the merest of margins. He spoke about his older brother Walter with great affection, telling me he was a gifted swimmer, much better than himself. Walter, unfortunately, had very poor eyesight, and could not serve in the regular armed forces, so he joined the "Home Guard." Ironically, drowning one dark night in the river Clyde right in the heart of Glasgow. He was on guard duty in the docks when it was attacked by German bombers, a blast from one of the bombs threw him into the water and he did not survive.

On Saturday mornings Dad would take me to Rolf Street Baths, teaching me to swim. This was only a few minutes' walk from Gran's house, unfortunately swimming gave him ear trouble, so he used earplugs to protect them. On our first visit, he literally, "threw me in at the deep end" to get me to swim, it was a shock, but it worked. It was just a clumsy dog paddle at first, but I soon became a competent swimmer. In the changing cubicle, I can remember asking him "Where do babies come from?" maybe seeing him naked stirred something in my six-year-old subconscious mind. What he said has long been forgotten, but he must have deftly changed the subject, for I was none the wiser and never asked an adult that question again.

One piece of memorable advice he gave me was how to dry myself thoroughly, giving particular attention to the groin area. This still resonates in my mind when drying myself after bathing and has stood me in good stead over the years. Rolf Street Baths were sadly demolished many years ago, but like the Phoenix, it has risen again, and can now be seen at the Black Country Museum.

He never swam at the much bigger and more modern Thimble Mill Baths but did take me to swim there on a couple of occasions. This was much later, possibly under duress and pressure from my mother, to get me out of the house and from under her feet. He would sit impatiently waiting for me in the large refectory above the entrance. Its décor was very art deco, reminiscent of its prewar construction and everywhere was painted in the ubiquitous green and cream. I can see him there in my mind's eye, sitting in their green wicker refectory chairs, his elbows on their glass-surfaced, green wicker tables, sipping weak tea, looking bored, sad, miserable, and irritable. Being a burden and repressing someone else's life was apparent to me even at my tender age.

On one, visit I can remember the pair of us looking down at the very small Police Station. It was immediately opposite the swimming baths and below the refectory and seeing hundreds of policemen marching along the road. Dad and I stared in amazement, and he said "I've never seen so many policemen, Johnny, what have you done?" we both laughed but I remain to this day puzzled, as to why so many police were marching from the little police station.

My first experience of a football match came in 1952, it was Uncle Reg a policeman who had organised the trip, he was married to Auntie Maud one of Mom's older sisters, West Bromwich Albion was playing Aston Villa away on Boxing Day. Dad took me to their house where transport in the form of a batted old van had been arranged. It was a one-all draw; all I remember was the miles of empty desolate concrete terraces and all the rubbish after the match. That was the only time Dad took me to a first-division game.

He always had a season ticket for West Bromwich Albion football club, it looked like a chequebook. He never took me to see a senior game but did take me once to a reserve match. This was just a practice game for unselected players or those recovering from injury, and they are very poorly attended. Coincidently there was always a bar open, so this would allow

Dad to quench his thirst, every Saturday during the season. What football team he supported I never knew, a guess would be "Glasgow Rangers", he never talked about them or any other football team or showed any real enthusiasm for the game. One day near Christmas he brought home a couple of large football books about West Bromwich Albion football club, he announced they had been signed by all their first-team players.

Proudly telling everyone, he was going to give them to Ronnie and Stuart my two cousins as Christmas presents, I was so disappointed; felt very undervalued. Their dad, Uncle Reg took them to every home game, so their love and understanding of the game was far more developed than mine. Never being taken to a first-team game has left me with a feeling of disappointment. It is only natural for a father to want to take his son with him. So, it left me with no understanding of its capacity to enthral and influence young boys. However, to be fair, if his motivation was just to find a watering hole then it's perfectly understandable.

Occasionally, we would play crazy golf and he usually won, in triumph he would sing "I'm the king of the castle and you're a dirty wee rascal" and we would all join in with his laughter. He often brought us ice creams and, on the way to make the purchase would sing "I scream you scream we all scream for ice cream" He loved boxing and would take me to amateur boxing matches at the Thimble Mill Baths. I always found it a bit scary. The booing and shouting, the violence, an atmosphere full of smoke, sweat, and charged with polarized alliances.

Chapter 7 At the Flicks

Back in our days in Smethwick, we had no television, Dad's main entertainment was radio and newspapers. The exception to this was our weekly visit to the Empire cinema, it was so close it's back almost reached into Gran's back garden. I can remember being in a state of excitement all day, every Thursday! This was the day they changed to a new film program, and it coincided with Dad's payday. They also added a short variety of live acts before the start of the film, it could be a singer, comedian, dancer, it was usually local talent and we all found it extremely entertaining. Early in his career, Charlie Chaplin had appeared there, I was shown the poster and there's evidence that he may have been born in Smethwick, at a gypsy encampment known as Black Patch.

To add to the seedy grandeur of the place they welcomed patrons by way of a very jolly commissionaire. He was dressed in a pseudo, military-type, claret-coloured uniform festooned with gold braid, and wore white gloves. At the time I thought he was very grand and important, one evening as Dad was taking us in, he asked, "Why do you only come on a Thursday?" Dad being quite reserved- hesitated in his reply, so being a precocious child, I butted in "Oh that's because dad gets paid on a Thursday" Later, I suffered painful retribution for interrupting him and causing embarrassment. Often a large group of us would go to the Empire, especially if a local act of some distinction was performing. One of our neighbours; was a fine operatic tenor, or so he thought. We all had to go and see him which I didn't fully appreciate.

One of the families that often accompanied us was the Jones's, the cobblers. They were on the corner of White Road, where it met the High Street in Smethwick, only about a hundred yards from Gran's house. Mr. Jones the Cobbler had a daughter called Betty and she was a close friend of Mom's. One of her brothers was married to Rita, she dazzled me, she was Greek, I think it was a wartime romance. She always wore brightly coloured dresses, and was happy, laughing, and smiling. Her voice was full of excitement, resonating with the most exotic accent, she was highly mobile, small, and petite. Sonya and I received most of her attention, unlike most adults who often seemed very distant. Dropping down to our level, saying something funny, her white teeth flashing a great smile, her raven black hair sweeping the line of our vision revealing her great circular earrings, she added allure, to the excitement of the occasion. Also, Uncle Eric came with us on at least one occasion, I remember him teaching me a comical rhyme about a turkey, which I've never forgotten. He was married to Mom's sister Auntie Flo, and they had one son, Cousin Robert, who now resides in the USA, it's possible they came with us too. Their marriage ended a few years later and so he disappeared from my life after that, as people often do. His son kept me informed of his well-being over the years, and he spent his final years living in Torquay, he will always remain a fun character to me.

Sadly, the Empire Cinema closed in the mid-1950s, television having a very detrimental effect on the popularity of movie theatres. Several of our favourite cinemas soldiered on bravely for a few more years, the Princess Hall, and the Beacon in Smethwick, and the Gaumont in Cape Hill. The Odeon,

Danilo, and Majestic were also added to our list when we moved to our new house in Quinton.

Together Dad, and I watched most of the major films of the late 1940s and 1950s mainly war or cowboy films. Sonya occasionally came if a more general film was playing. Listed here are just a few of the more memorable ones, "On the Waterfront, High Noon, The Dam Busters, Morlon Rouge, and possibly our final film The Yangtse Incident."

Dad would tell me we were going to the pictures that night and name the cinema and the time. Then all day I would be excitedly watching the clock slowly ticking away, hardly able to contain myself till at last the magic moment arrived. When we lived in Smethwick most of the cinemas were within easy walking distance but after moving, we would catch the bus and wait for him outside the designated cinema. Once, and maybe towards the end of his life, he "stood us up!" We waited and waited, it seemed like hours, we couldn't believe that Dad had forgotten us, but he had. It hurt deeply, he probably got sidetracked in some pub. We caught the bus home, disappointed and dejected.

Chapter 8 Critical Times

Walking with Dad on Brasshouse Lane one day we crossed a bridge that spans two canals, the drop from the bridge to the water below is considerable. Innocently, I mentioned that for a dare, our gang would climb upon the high wall and walk that way to cross the bridge. Dad went very pale I'd never seen him change colour so quickly! He told me off, warning me of the grave dangers involved. After that, I can never remember being encouraged by the gang to cross that way again, maybe he spoke to their parents.

There is one memory that I can very accurately date, on the 6th of February 1952, I was standing in front of Gran's radio in the living room. The newsreader sadly announced that the king had died, I started crying, and just then Dad came down the stairs, into the living room. He asked, "Why are you crying?" I replied, "The king has died!" his response was "You silly bugger" When the Coronation of Queen Elizabeth was being broadcast on the 2nd of June 1953, we all went round to Mrs. Shepherds next door and watched it on her new T.V. Later we went to the street party arranged by the locals and had a great time.

In the early days, Dad did seem more at ease with family life, the calming influence of Grandma may have been an important factor. On most evenings just before bedtime, relaxing in his armchair by the open fire he would call me over, put me on his lap, and read to me various boys' adventure stories.

One particularly comes to mind; Treasure Island, this memorable event was further reinforced when he took me to see the Disney film of the book which was released on the 13th of July 1950. When reading the newspaper, he would often comment on events or headlines, I remember the famous picture of Stalin lying in an open coffin at his state funeral, and the end of the Korean War, both events happening in 1953.

Around that time, I was told he borrowed a moped with a tiny motor, its lack of power meant at times you needed to pedal to keep it going, especially up hills. It's difficult to believe, but he used it to go and see his folks in Scotland. How long he took, and the details of the journey are long forgotten but he must have been fit to accomplish such a journey. About this time, he may have tried his hand at carpentry and had some evening lessons. Several interesting wooden items in various stages of completion appeared, a boat needing some remedial work, a round beautifully turned light with a glazed frosted front about the size and shape of a dinner plate, and an art deco-style wooden wall clock with electric workings, about the size and shape of a family bible. The only item that was ever put into use was the clock, it needed a permanent electrical supply, so Dad wired it up and put it above the mantelpiece in the sitting room. What happened to this, and the other items is not on record.

There were bitter arguments between Mom and Dad when she told him she had decided to get a job as a barmaid at the Crown pub on the High Street, in Smethwick, I'm not sure if she did evenings, but I know she did mornings and lunchtime. One day when I was four or five years old, I decided to wait outside the pub and walk home with her.

When she saw me, she became very angry and told me in no uncertain terms, I was showing her up! And to never wait for her again. Pointing across the road, she ordered me to go over there and to walk on the other side. My scruffy appearance was apparently, giving people the wrong impression! In later years, I was reminiscing with my sister Sonya and mentioned the incident and the hurt I'd felt. Sonya was well known for being unable to keep a confidence. Therefore, I wasn't too surprised when she repeated what I'd said to Mom. What did shock me, however, was Mom's response. Instead of the expected denial, and debunking my memory, she concurred with the story and found it extremely funny.

Mum arranged a holiday for us at the seaside in 1951, staying at her sister's boarding house in Paignton in the county of Devon. It was called the Tree Tops Hotel, Dad couldn't come with us because he was too busy stocktaking. Whether this was true, or he was just trying to obtain a little respite from the rigors of family life, I do not know. But even as a five-year-old, I was suspicious of his motives. The three of us, Mom, Sonya, and me, were picked up by a friend of hers, he owned a very elegant, Triumph Mayflower car, all shinney and black. It was with a feeling of sadness, leaving Dad behind it just didn't feel right to me.

His job in buying was unfortunately undermined by what we would call today, unprofessional or unethical practices. Suppliers would send gifts to influence buyers, dependent on the status of the buyer and the size of their potential expenditure. This would determine both the quantity and value of the gifts. I can remember seeing at grandma's house, huge boxes containing thousands of John Player cigarettes, a very expensive brand. Watching his face light up with joy as he opened these exclusive navy-blue cardboard boxes, with the John Player logo in one corner. They were the size of large chocolate boxes containing hundreds of fat, white, round cigarettes. He would then grab a fistful, decanting them down into smaller more practical packets. As time passed it seemed to grow in volume and variety, especially when he went to work at Phillips Cycles, his final employer, where possibly his status improved even more. The giving of gifts to gain influence was widespread throughout the commercial world and seen as one of the perks of the job. It was greatly curtailed, by the government removing some of the tax advantages associated with the practice, but this was long after Dad had passed. The range of gifts was quite extensive, soap products of all kinds and kitchenware, but the most common were large quantities of whiskey and cigarettes. These would be delivered nearly every day, the cupboard stacked with rows of whiskey bottles and boxes of cigarettes.

Chapter 9 Great Changes

On our journeys to West Smethwick Park from grandma's, which was at the most a fifteen-minute walk, I can remember him pointing out Ronnie Allen's very modest house, a typical semidetached home built between the wars. He was a very famous football player, in those days even the top players needed to earn extra money, especially in the off-season. He used to sell Industrial Brushes and call on Dad in his capacity as a Buyer, in the hope of selling them. In today's football world, he would be a multi-millionaire, and the need to add income in this way would seem ridiculous. How things have changed!

Mom and Dad began preparations to emigrate to Canada where some of our Scottish relatives had settled. Sonya and I knew very little about it, we did however notice some correspondence with them. We were told they were helping to prepare the requirements for our departure. All this; was put on hold when Mom became pregnant with Scott, he was born on the 6th of April 1953. In the meantime, maybe our prospects had improved for the better, because the subject faded away never to be mentioned again.

Exactly one year after his birth, we were given a brand-new council house in an area known as Quinton, on the outskirts of Birmingham. When the great day came to move in, we were all very excited. It all seemed so wonderful; little did I realize the massive changes that were ahead of us. Some were positive many were not! Dad and Mom worked feverishly, together with Uncle Reg putting all our worldly goods in a removal van and then unloading them at our new house. It was also Scott's first birthday, I remember holding him on my lap, looking through the van window, pointing out our new home. It was the 6th of April 1954 two major events happening, all in one day! The adults were puffing, panting, and sweating profusely, luckily the weather was on their side, very typically British, cold, wet, and windy. One incident, that could have been disastrous was perpetrated by me, it happened as we were about to depart. Under Gran's stairs there was a long dark cupboard, full of mysterious objects, together with a multitude of dust and cobwebs. Stuffed in there were such items as World War 2 gas masks, and old tin hats, to explore this, I took a burning candle, and left it there still alight. Thankfully, the ensuing fire was extinguished before too much damage was done. The distraction of moving home; could also have saved me from receiving too much punishment for this careless act.

Our brand-new house was brick built with three bedrooms, semidetached of modern design, at 132, Bleakhouse Road, Birmingham 32. It had a sizable garden and a separate solid brick-built outhouse. Also, a bathroom and inside toilet! these would seem very normal today but back then it was a wonderful luxury. We could now dispense with foul-smelling chamber pots stuffed under the bed, and the odour of stale urine would be a thing of the past. We could now bathe anytime, without the need to bring in the tin bath from outside.

Thank goodness, the day was over when you needed to boil endless saucepans, and wait for your turn to bathe in grey, oily-looking, second-hand water and only once a week on "Bath Night." It was all so exciting; little did I know I had only four years left with Dad before he would succumb to Coronary thrombosis. So much happened, in that short time, as I look back, we did so much together, I don't think a lifetime could yield more.

There was an embarrassing situation that year, the time of Cousin Brian Viney's wedding. His younger brother Arnold was "doing his national service" in the army, and on leave for the big day. He had a girlfriend who lived in Smethwick, she accompanied him to the wedding. She was slim, petite with long blonde hair, and very attractive. She can be seen in a large group photograph, which I believe was taken at the wedding reception, she is sitting just behind Mom and Dad. In a damaged fragment I have, (a close-up from this picture) you can just see her arm almost touching Dad's left shoulder. What exactly happened I do not know, I would have been only eight at the time, but what I know for certain is there was a horrendous row between Mom and Dad, also Arnold was involved. There was even a journey to this young lady's house, the adults going in, Sonya and I sitting outside waiting in a car. After which, as far as I was concerned, the matter was brushed under the carpet. Mother never talked about it, and although I got to know Arnold very well in later years, he never mentioned it.

It was not long after we had settled into our new home, that trouble between Mom and Dad began to intensify, public house hours were very strictly controlled in those days. He would drink at the pub on a Sunday lunchtime, then return home for his dinner, after this he would dose- off and wake refreshed. At about 6 pm he would become cheerful and happy; I remember Mom saying, "Look at him, he's getting happy now it's near opening time" This would start a row. He would then leave for the pub, slamming the door. Mom would run to the window and begin banging on it with the side of her clenched fist, almost to breaking point. Then throw it open and shout insults for the neighbours to hear. All this, as he walked nonchalantly up to the pub just a few minutes' walk away. On at least one occasion she even went into the pub and admonished him in front of his drinking pals, telling him his dinner was on the table.

One fine sunny morning, just after we'd moved to our new house, Mom announced she'd had enough, and we were leaving Dad. It was all very dramatic; Dad was on his knees laying a path in the middle of the garden. Without, any prior warning, we were all taken down to say goodbye to him. He never got up, just meekly turned towards us and smiled a sad sorrowful smile. Mom turned round and flounced off, and we followed her to catch the bus to Grandma's, poor old Gran what she had to put up with! The problem for Sonya and me was that we had moved schools, from Devonshire Road School to Tipton Road School. Our old school was just a few minutes' walk from Grans, now we had to catch a bus to our new school, making the journey much more inconvenient. Luckily, this spat only lasted for a few days, and we returned to Dad, the new house, and to ride on the school bus which conveniently pulled up, right outside our house. Sadly, the new path was never finished, the base for the final slab was in place but it never came. Why? I do not know, but for years after we used to fill the large gap with water and frogspawn, studying the resultant developments with great interest.

Dad had a small, battered leather case in the shed in which he kept his set of tools, there was the usual hammer, screwdrivers, and my favourite the hand drill, it had a lovely polished wooden handle and a largish orange painted gear wheel with a handle to turn it, this rotated a small cog on a shaft on to which a collet was attached. Into this, you placed your drill bit, enabling you to carry out a wide range of DIY jobs, such as putting up shelves. He should have locked it away or hidden it from me. The tools were my playthings. Especially the hand drill, it substituted for a Bren-Gun or Sci-Fi Ray gun. Soon all the tools were lost leaving an empty case, he must have been frustrated and demotivated by my irritating behaviour. Today, I would have been labelled with one of those psychological issues like ADHD. More than once, I believe Mom and Dad discussed my mental and behavioural problems.

Despite all the setbacks, he did find some motivation, in those early days at our new home. He brought huge tins of very dark varnish and painted all the bare pine floorboards in the house. He worked very hard I can see him now, on his knees furiously painting away, beads of sweat on his forehead. He was probably very proud when he'd finished, it was very much the fashion at the time, but today would seem far too dull.

Mom and Dad must have been good dancers, on one of their rare evenings out together, they came home happy and smiling. Proudly showing off a bottle of apricot brandy they'd just won in a dancing competition.

Chapter 10 Holidays and Health

In his new job as a Buyer for Phillips Cycles, one of his suppliers was the Shell oil company. Their representative was extremely friendly with Dad. Whether it was a genuine friendship or just a commercial one is difficult to say, but he did visit our home from time to time. On one occasion I swapped a rowing machine for a tent with him. He had offered or was persuaded to chauffer our family to Paignton, for a fortnight's holiday at Auntie Flo`s guest house. It was 1955 so there would have been six of us including the new addition – Ross, who would only be a few months old, it was quite a squeeze!

We arrived late afternoon, it was cool and overcast with a bit of a chilly breeze, a typical English summer day. Despite the conditions, I immediately wanted to swim and pestered Dad to take me. He said he was too busy and had to help unpack; fortunately, the kind driver, his friend offered to take me, saying he'd brought his swimming kit and wanted a swim himself. So, while all business of settling in was taking place, I was excitedly going for a swim, The man's name escapes me, but he talked about his two sons, one was about my age, and I found him warm and friendly. We swam in the sea for a while then we went onto the pier, by then I was cold and shivering still in my swimming trunks. He purchased for us a hot cup of tea and a Cornish Pasty, to this day I have never tasted a better one. Over the years I've enjoyed the pleasure of many a pasty but never found its equal. The man was so different from my dad, I supposed that all men were taciturn, strict, serious, and slightly disinterested like my dad.

This guy made me feel important, the centre of attention, he joked, and he chatted, I'd never experienced that before. He may have been very different with his children, after all, I was the child of a customer, and keeping me happy helped business.

Later in the holiday, Dad, Sonya, and I went swimming, Dad wearing his special black swimming hat, it had little suckers on the inside trying to seal out the water, but he also wore earplugs as a second line of defence. Seeing him power through the water, pushing a small tsunami in front of him I realised that he was a very powerful and competent swimmer.

Dad and I spent quite some time together that holiday, one day he decided to go sea-fishing. We went down to the harbour, and he hired a boat, an open rowing boat, like the one's on park pools, only slightly larger. In the middle was a large box containing the diesel engine, which you started with a handle, turning vigorously till it coughed and spluttered into life. Smoke and fumes filling the air, soon clearing as we moved away. The boat also came with two oars just in case the engine stopped, and importantly the fishing tackle. This comprised of two lines wound around a wooden frame, at their ends were shiny metal spinners and attached to them fishing hooks. They looked very much like large dangly earrings, only they spun with the forward motion of the boat, sunlight flashing on their chrome surfaces attracting the fish to bite. We started catching fish almost straightaway, at first, I was traumatised by their flapping about and having to remove hooks from their mouths. Dad soon showed the way by grasping them firmly, unhooking them, and throwing them gasping in a corner of the boat.

They soon began to pile-up and I became very gratified by our work. When we returned to the harbour Dad, allowed me to carry the catch back to the "Guest House." It's said that "Pride comes before a fall" and puffed up with it, I went straight to the kitchen. Where Auntie Flo and Mom were chatting, presenting them proudly, with my prize, a sack full of freshly caught fish. They both were extremely underwhelmed; I was completely deflated. My expectations of being praised and lauded for my great prowess were destroyed. Auntie Flo said, "What do you expect me to do with them" It was apparent that Mackerel were not going to be on the menu at the Tree Tops Hotel.

Dad and I went on a few more fishing trips in Torbay in similar boats. What happened to the catches I can't remember, I certainly didn't present them to Auntie Flo, possibly gave them away at the quay. Later she very much redeemed herself in my eyes, after the incident with the fish, calling me into the kitchen and presenting me with a lemon Méringue pie. It was like tasting a piece of heaven and remains my favourite dessert to this day.

Our final trip out in Torbay was unforgettable, unfortunately, there were no boats with engines available. So, Dad decided to take out the unpowered rowing boat, that he had been offered. A calm sea and a blue sky greeted us with a gentle breeze blowing in from the southwest, giving perfect conditions. The tide helped us get underway and soon we were out of the sight of land. The lines were out, and we were happily catching fish and time was passing quickly. Health and safety in those days were taken far less seriously, we had no life jackets just a couple of balers, used mainly to relieve ourselves, throwing the contents overboard. Standing up in a rowing boat for a pee can be very precarious.

In no time at all, and at great speed the weather began to change. Ominous black clouds began to gather, and the breeze stiffened changing into a howling wind. Dad calmly ordered the lines to be wound in and began rowing steadily towards land, hopefully in the right direction, and to the safety of the harbour. The sea then began to buckle and roll and seemed to change from an attractive bluey green into a threatening grey, edged with flecks of white foam. The boat at one moment was diving down a steep slope into an endless grim valley, then climbing almost vertically towards the black sky. I began to cry, baling furiously as the sea poured - in, terrified thinking we were going to be swamped. Laughing, Dad shouted out "Johnny when you`ve rowed boats in the Scottish Islands this is nothing, just keep bailing" Immediately, I calmed down and kept bailing, thankfully we eventually made it safely back to dry land.

One night during the holiday Mom, Dad, and Auntie Flo went to a Ball at the nearby prestigious hotel. It all got slightly out of hand when Mom accused her sister of being too familiar with Dad. Mom and Auntie Flo often argued. Mom was difficult, ultra-sensitive, and could enjoy a joke played on someone else but couldn't take a joke on herself. Flo was broad-minded, earthy, and more self-deprecating. Dad would have been very comfortable with Auntie Flo they both liked a drink and knew how to relax.

One morning towards the end of our fortnight holiday a commotion occurred near the bathroom, the door was locked and whoever was in there wasn't answering. The lock was forced but something was blocking the door, it was Dad's body lying on the floor. They called an ambulance and eventually managed to release the door and take Dad to the hospital.

He had had a stroke; he was only thirty-eight. His mouth drooped and the right side of his body was partially paralysed. His speech was slurred, and he found it difficult to communicate, he was very frightened and emotional. It was the first time I realised his vulnerability, after all, he was my hero and indestructible. Mom told our next-door neighbour, Mrs. Stevens, that he clung to her in his hospital bed, crying in fear of death, mockingly she questioned his manliness and seemed pleased he was now weak and dependent.

How we returned with Dad from our holiday has long been forgotten, possibly the good man from Shell gave his support to aid our return. Shortly after, Dad had another stroke, which I believe often happens. The first I knew of it was an ambulance parked outside the house, Dad in his pyjamas being carried away on a stretcher, the blanket nearly slipping off, the neighbours gathering around, Dad with an embarrassed smile on his face. It was heartbreaking to see him so reduced, his pride broken, his modesty and privacy invaded. Mom: said that the doctor had told her that the hot sun on his balding pate, may have participated in bringing on the first stroke. He was, however, overweight, well over sixteen stone. He drank and smoked heavily; his drinking was getting out of control eventually to the level of a bottle of whiskey daily. His heavy drinking had likely turned him into an alcoholic, but at what stage the transition occurred I do not know. His doctor did warn him of the consequences of his lifestyle and where it would lead him.

His recovery was remarkably fast, and my fears began to rapidly abate, his resilience was remarkable. His face and speech quickly returned to normal, his right-side paralysis disappeared, and for all intents and purposes, he was back to his old self.

He returned to work, and he was talking about buying a car, I remember him discussing with Uncle Charlie, the difficulties he was having trying to obtain car insurance. Maybe he helped Dad, because his illness would have detrimentally affected the chances of him obtaining suitable cover.

Chapter 11 Material Growth

Shortly after moving, we began to gain considerably in material wealth. I can only assume it was when he'd changed employers and began working at Phillips Cycles. Overhearing Dad and Mom speaking one day, a figure of eighteen pounds a week was mentioned. Which was a very good salary and in 1954 would be quite substantial. It is about thirty-three thousand pounds per annum, in today's money. This may not sound very much now, but it was double the average wage of nine pounds forty-five pence, in 1954. Doubling the average wage today, you would need to earn over seventy thousand pounds per annum, a very reasonable income.

One of Dad's first big buys was a television set. The model was heavily advertised on Radio Luxenberg, one of his favourite stations. It was a "Pye, Picture Controlled, Television Set", with a fourteen-inch black and white screen. In 1955 there came a significant change to the television world, up till then, there was only one channel the B.B.C. The government finally allowed independent television broadcasts, so Dad installed a special electronic device to receive them. It was a brown plastic box, screwed to the side of the T.V. controlled by a rotating switch with channel numbers on them. I was very impressed by Dad's ability to convert the T.V.

from a single channel (BBC) to a multi-channel set. He also purchased a self-build television table, which he constructed and varnished to give a polished finish. You still see them come up for sale on rare occasions, in charity shops.

His new company had a sizable canteen, possibly with a stage area, although I never saw it. I am assuming this because it was going to be used by the newly formed independent television company I.T.V. to host one of its shows "Hit the Limit" and what's more Dad was going to be on it! The show ran from 1956 to 1957 and was hosted at works canteens all around the Midlands area, Pete Murry was one of its several presenters. He commented in later years, "It may well have been the worst program ever on television" he also mentioned, "what exactly the format was, nobody quite knew" that was at the time, so today it's even more obscure. It was roughly like this; a dart was thrown at a rotating dart board, it was about six feet in diameter, and painted on it were several segments, each with a cash prize, ascending in value. The star prize was £250.00; after the dart was thrown, you were required to answer three general knowledge questions, to receive the money in the segment your dart hit. If you answered them correctly you were given the cash, otherwise you had to do a forfeit. Singing, dancing, or some other trial. After all that, you were paid something for your trouble, exactly how the amount was calculated is now thankfully lost in the mists of time. To enhance the show, a celebrity came in halfway through to add some respite, I believe Mel Torma` an American singer, nicknamed `The Velvet Fog` was the act that night, dad told us that after the show he had a drink at the bar with him.

We all sat around the television waiting for the programme to start, excitement and tension became unbearable, we couldn't wait to see Dad on the TV, but he didn't appear! I don't think I've ever experienced a greater anticlimax, Dad was disappointed too, but remained cheerful. He told us time had run out to get him on the show, but the presenter Jerry Desmond, famous for being the straight man in several Norman Wisdom films, promised him the first spot on the following week's show. Sure enough, the promise was kept, and there was Dad on television, we could hardly believe what we were seeing.

It was all very jocular dad threw his dart, failed to answer all the questions correctly, and had to do his forfeit. It was an Apache dance, a Parisian Street scene with accordion music was the background; and a sexy-looking woman came wriggling on and danced with Dad, she drew a knife trying to stab him, and suddenly disappeared when Dad flung her away. The presenter then came up to Dad and gave him his prize of £7.00. Later Dad told us he'd got too carried away with his part; using so much force in the last move that his dancing partner fell into the scenery.

Sonya and I over the years often reminisced about Dad's appearance on TV and agreed how wonderful it would be if a copy still existed. Unfortunately, most television programmes in those days were not recorded, and have disappeared into the ether. It was too expensive then to make and keep copies, so unless they were on film, none have survived.

It was so exciting when he first tuned in to those independent television broadcasts. To watch commercial adverts with their so-called "jingles" and to enjoy their more popularist programming. So much in contrast to the stuffy middle-class outpourings of the B.B.C.

We watched quite a lot of television programs together, the big Alexander Korda movies. The special half-hour adventure shorts, such as Robin Hood with Richard Green, Ivanhoe with Roger Moore, Sir Lancelot with William Russell, amazingly he is still alive at the time of writing, at 98 years, Dad's biggest favourite was Highway Patrol starring Brodrick Crawford, famous for the call sign "Ten-4". It was a very action-packed American, police drama.

Shortly after the television's arrival, the living room caught fire, Mom had left clothes drying around an open coal fire, the heat causing them to catch fire. Scott would have been about three and Ross about eighteen months old, they were in great danger, shut in the room. Luckily, Mom returned and quickly extinguished the fire before it harmed the children. The damage to the room was light, the flames had scorched one side of the television set damaging its glossy varnish finish, and causing a permanent black streak but this wasn't too noticeable. The radio set, resting on top had its woven colourful plastic speaker cover partly melt, but it still worked. Unfortunately, Dad's photograph, displayed on the very top was destroyed. It was a black-and-white, studio-type portrait picture of high quality. Showing him in his R.A.F. uniform looking very young and handsome. It was the only copy and the only professional photograph of him in his prime.

The next significant purchase was a Hotpoint Empress washing machine, it was a huge, heavy, cream-coloured, rectangular washer. Stowed away in a cupboard at its base, was a heavy electric mangle which you lifted and fixed into the top. Used, after the wash was finished, many people must have damaged their backs lifting it into position. Nevertheless, it must have been a boon to Mom with her ever-expanding brood. In the mid 50's very few ordinary people owned such luxuries, they were so expensive, and this model would have cost nearly two thousand pounds in today's money. Years later, when she acquired a more modern washer, she asked me to dispose of it. I was working in the machine shop of a large factory and asked around, "Was anybody interested?" Surprisingly a guy said he would buy it and collected it from Mom's house. I was a little nervous, because of its age and heavy usage, there could be problems! My fears abated a few weeks later; when he slapped me on the shoulder and told me it was a great machine and a bargain buy.

The next exciting addition to our home was a large glossy radiogram. It came together with loads of modern vinal records, and it had a B.S.R. automatic turntable. Dad's favourite singer was Eartha Kitt and he brought several of her records. Dating this period accurately is quite easy because the smash hit "Walking in the Rain" sung by Johnny Rae was topping the charts in 1956. We pestered Dad to get us a copy, but he only brought a cover version, we were very disappointed, hope it didn't show.

That year he also bought a black Morris Oxford car, registration number KOH 731. It was very similar to the iconic Morris Minor only bigger. He had only a provisional driving licence and had to display learner plates. The onset of the Suez crisis may have motivated him because the government postponed driving tests from October 1956 to April 1957 to save fuel, and learners were allowed to drive unaccompanied. He never passed his test, although he tried a few times. His health may have had a major impact, preventing him from performing tasks to the required standards.

This creates a bit of a puzzle, because in his RAF papers his occupation before his enlistment, in March 1937 was "Van Driver" and compulsory testing began in June 1935. Maybe he needed to renew his Driving Licence more often and during his time in the RAF he didn't bother, so it ran out.

In 1956 it was quite something to own a car. You could determine quite accurately the wealth and status of its owner. The majority of people didn't own one, so, I felt very important and puffed up with pride sitting in Dad's car. Occasionally, waving at my reflection in shop windows pretending to be royalty.

Often, Dad would take me out on a Sunday afternoon to the Clent Hills, or Bewdley. I can remember being all warm and cosy, protected from the elements as the rain lashed down. Looking at a huge Guinness sign with its iconic and colourful picture of a Toucan. It was displayed under the railway bridge at Bewdley. Enjoying the amusing cleverness of `Gilroy`s artwork, and sitting in Dad`s parked car, patiently waiting for him. While he obtained some libation from the several pubs in its locality. Many things have changed since then but amazingly the advertising hoarding is still there. Under the railway bridge at Bewdley, nearly seventy years later. On one of these trips, it was an unusually hot day, with a heat haze coming off the road, giving that mirage effect of approaching a lake, Dad with a look of mischief on his face "began to shove the pedal to the metal" he then said excitedly "Johnny look at the speedo" we were flat-out, possibly just scraping seventy miles an hour and both laughing.

After buying the car, occasionally he would take me along to a vehicle scrap yard. Here, he would search for replacement spares to keep his car running, but he must have given the work to a local mechanic because I never saw him doing any repairs himself. That scrap yard or second-hand car parts replacement business surprisingly still exists after all these years, on the same site, and is called; First Warley Motor Salvage Breakers, in Tipton Road Oldbury, West Midlands. The site was quite extensive in Dad's time, but housing developments have shrunk it to a much smaller area. The present occupier of the site had some very poor reviews on their performance. I hope in Dad's time things were much better, and he didn't need to make similar complaints.

One day the house filled with antiques of every kind imaginable. There was a large dining table and chairs, a very elegant bureau, loads of silver cutlery, statues, and many other items now forgotten. Dad said he'd brought them at an auction. Included in the "Job Lot" was a large bronze statue of a Chinese gentleman. He was holding a fishing rod and dressed in traditional Chinese clothes, perched on a huge rock. He was enjoying a day's fishing and giving the impression he was shaking with laughter. It had been placed on top of the hall cupboard and I passed it on my way to school. Running down the hall, I would slap his leering face, in revenge. It made me angry, he appeared to be sadistically gaining pleasure and mocking me for having to go to school.

Chapter12 Heartbreak and Generosity

One dull miserable Saturday, in the month of May 1956 the peace and tranquillity of our home was broken by a loud knocking on the front door, a smart young man riding a motorcycle in a post office uniform was delivering a telegram addressed to Dad. We all gathered in the hall witnessing this dramatic scene. The grownups had very grim expressions on their faces, we were bemused, not understanding why this unusual and exciting event had caused such a reaction. We did not realise, at the time, but such deliveries rarely brought good news. Dad feverishly tore it open, read its contents, and immediately let out a heart-rending sob of pain and anguish, I had never seen him so utterly distraught, and just for a moment, his veil of masculine persona fell. Showing the vulnerable and tender man he was, and I did not know. Running up the stairs crying unashamedly, he disappeared to his room and remained there for a considerable time. The bad news was his sister Agnus had just died at the age of forty-nine, a cerebral haemorrhage was stated as the cause of death. She was eleven years older than Dad, so she may have been like a second mother to him. Supporting her mum in the care and protection of the younger children, it's only conjecture but this may have created a very strong bond between them.

One evening he came home from work; I was sitting down engrossed in some television programme. He put his head round the door and said, "Johnny! there's something for you outside, go and take a look." Leaning on the sidewall of the house was a brand-new bicycle! All wrapped up in brown paper packaging. I cannot remember a time in my life when I was more excited and overcome with gratitude. He smiled with pleasure at my reaction and watched as I painstakingly removed the wrapping, it was mainly a metallic red with blue with white lettering and called by Phillips "The Valiant" after I'd supposed, the famous delta-winged aircraft of that time. This misapprehension stayed with me all these years, till I did research for this book. The name had been used on various models by Phillips for years, well before the aircraft became famous. It was slightly too big for me, and he was concerned for my safety so took me out several times, observing my riding skills. Climbing onto the bike for the first time, I used a little wall in front of our house to steady myself. Dad holding the back of the saddle. He said, "Ok you can go now" and I wobbled off down the sloping path. He wasn't happy with my performance and told me so, I was bitterly disappointed. He strongly advised me that I needed to vastly improve. And if I did, he would allow me to use it without his permission. After several tutorials, he gave me the OK, letting me go and use it as I wished. Although I'm guessing that he probably got bored, or just gave up on a hopeless case, on today's roads I possibly wouldn't have survived.

His tolerance was inconsistent he never hit Sonya and I never even heard him verbally chastise her, or the other children for that matter. It was for me, on the other hand quite different, and I was subject to quite a considerable amount of chastisement, both verbal and physical. Children can be intensely annoying; on this scale, I must have been at the extreme end. Sonya would often recall with great amusement, that we'd all be watching T.V. eating sweets, and I would be loudly smacking my lips. Unaware of the annoyance, it was causing in my vicinity. Suddenly, without warning I would be knocked from my chair with a swipe from Dad's hand, telling me to shut up.

Once in a severe snowstorm, I was trying to knock snowflakes off the front window using a hand brush and smashed it. Dad went off through the storm on the bus, it was before we had a car, and returned with a pane of glass, replacing it without any complaint. On another occasion, he sat in his chair and refused to speak to Mr. Nevitt, and I was never admonished for my behaviour. He was the owner of a local Newsagents and had come to report to Dad. That, I with a gang of lads, had climbed over his wall, stealing bottles of pop. Mr Nevitt told me he wanted to speak with Dad and sent me into the house to fetch him, and then began to cry when I told him that Dad had refused to speak to him. So, I went back into the house and reported that Mr. Nevitt was crying, Dad just shrugged his shoulders and said, "That's his problem!" I'd never seen a grown man cry and it completely shamed me, I never behaved like this again. A few years later Mr Nevett employed me as a Paperboy.

There was one time, when I was in the front bedroom, messing about with the light switch. Using it to transmit a long message in my version of the Morse code, it was to some unknown alien on a distant planet. Unbeknown to me Dad was walking down the path, returning home from work, and must have had a bad day. He pushed me down the stairs, punched me to the floor, and then began kicking me with Mom screaming "Leave him alone John! you`ll kill him."

He would also similarly attack Mom, nearly always when he`d been drinking, one night I was playing out late with a friend near the local phone box. Mom came running to up the phone box in her dressing gown and slippers. She was in a panic and crying, we stood back in the shadows she didn't see us. Later I found out that Dad had attacked her, and she rang her sister, Auntie Doll for support. In the past, on several occasions, she had reported him to the police but in those days, they put it down as "A Domestic", so no further action was taken.

More than once he left her in financial difficulties, and I can remember her at breakfast time asking him for money and explaining the reasons. This would lead to an argument, with Dad leaving for work and Mom running up the hall, begging for money before he left. I can see him now, half-turn, a scowl of disgust on his face, one hand on the door latch the other scattering money, Mom scurrying along the floor gathering it up like some beggar. It made me feel sorry for her needing to grovel like this, for what was needed, and angry with Dad for his bad behaviour.

Chapter 13 Too Little Too Late

He did try to break the cycle of habits that were threatening his health. Soon the cupboards were full of dietary food supplements, and he began taking long walks. Fortunately, he took me along with him and we walked for miles, he chose a variety of directions once along the Hagley Road into Birmingham and one time into Halesowen. On one of these walks, I remember crossing Warley Woods golf course, passing the old abbey, which was used as a clubhouse, he said "Johnny, if you want to be rich, take up golf," although I never forgot the advice, sadly the opportunity, never arose. This was all part of his new fitness regime which lasted for several months, the walks took place, usually on a Sunday evening. He was never very talkative in my company and there were times when he hardly spoke a word, I believe this may have affected my abhorrence for long silences. To ameliorate this, I would chatter away. Possibly I saw these silences as anger, and it made me fearful, but my immaturity, and underdeveloped empathy, made me ignorant of the inner demons that might be affecting him.

The walks gradually petered out and he went back to his old ways, gaining weight, smoking, and drinking heavily. In a relatively short time, he aged significantly, becoming rotund, haggard, and slow, using the car even for the shortest of journeys.

Sitting in the car, on one occasion Dad dug into his pocket and said "Here Johnny this is for you" he handed me a circular aluminium disc, like a large medallion at its very centre was a bright shiny farthing. On the aluminium outer face were stamped the words "As Long as you have me you will never be broke" They stopped producing it after 1956 and the farthing became illegal tender shortly after. It was a very Scottish gift indeed, I wondered why he was laughing when he gave it to me, and when I think of it today, it makes me smile.

One Saturday morning that year he took me to the Bull Ring in Birmingham; it was at the time just a shattered shell after being bombed during World War Two. It had to wait till the early 1960s to be rebuilt. All that remained was a circle broken of walls. They surrounded a large open area used as a marketplace, selling everything you can imagine. We went to the pet stall and Dad brought me a white mouse I kept in the garden shed, what happened to it is sadly forgotten. While in the city we visited the Hall of Memory a white stone building in the centre, once we had entered it, he became very serious and respectful. He told me that the names of all the people from here, who had lost their lives on active service, in the First and Second World Wars were recorded in there. It was a very treasured and solemn moment and although I have never returned, when I pass it on Broad Street, I always think of him and that special occasion. What his thoughts and emotions were during his visit I can only surmise, but over 50,000 young R.A.F. men were killed in the Second World War. He possibly knew many that never returned, and their average age would have been just twenty-three.

A very memorable day was when he took me on a trip to an industrial exhibition at Bingley Hall, Birmingham. It was famous in those days for holding important events on various themes. Such as cars, food, building materials, household materials, interior design, and many more, so I was very excited and proud Dad was taking me. At its rear, a railway carriage restaurant car had been drawn up to provide food for special guests, and he had been invited by one of his suppliers. It was such a revelation, all the tables beautifully laid out in white linen with silver service and the waiters so grand in their tails with white starched collars and ties. What I remember most was the bowl of tomato soup it was delicious, but I dread to think what my table manners must have been like, I hope it didn't cause Dad too much embarrassment.

Bonfire night was always celebrated at the new house, at Gran's I can never remember any such festivities, maybe it wasn't allowed. She was always terrified of thunder and lightning, when I was very small with just the two of us in the house, if a thunderstorm started, she would run around panicking. Switching off the radio and turning all the mirrors to face the wall, she believed they'd attract lightning. She would then squeeze my hand tightly, still panicking, and the pair of us would run round to Mrs Shepherd's next door to shelter from the storm. The memory of this makes me suspect she disliked and feared all the flashes and bangs on Bonfire night.

At our new house, several weeks before the event I would start building up a secret stash of fireworks, under a loose floorboard I'd found in the front bedroom. Then, in the back garden, I would start building up a bonfire. In the early days, Dad would also catch the bug and become enthusiastic.

He also, purchased fireworks to supplement the few I'd managed to hoard, with baked potatoes, pop, and other delights it was a very enjoyable event. This sadly declined with his health, and in the later years, he would just give us money to go and buy them ourselves. Disappointingly usually too late, when all the shops had sold out! After one such event, I had probably eaten too much, got over-excited, and began to suffer stomach cramps. In the middle of the night, I was awakened by gripping pain and could find no relief. Dad showing great concern, ran me a hot bath and spent time to ensure I was finding some relief; I never forgot this kindness.

In my last year of junior school at the age of eleven I was given the leading role in the school play; it was called King Melon. The year would be 1957 Mom came along to watch it, and I could see her along with the rest of the Moms and Dads cheering and clapping loudly at the end of our performance. The only thing missing was Dad, he had not made the effort to come and see it but had stayed at home, sitting in his armchair watching television. He looked old, sad, and forlorn when I returned, so although I was hurt at his apparent lack of interest, I also felt sorry for him. He called me over and as I stood by the arm of his chair, he smiled weakly and said well-done son and gave me two shillings. It was something of an approval but not enough to fill the void of disappointment I'd felt over his indifference to my big moment. In retrospect, his failing health may have been a significant factor, so I was probably being unfair not having the maturity to comprehend what he knew only too well; that for him time was running out.

Occasionally, Dad would have an evening at home. When it was my bedtime, and I was just about to say goodnight and leave the room. He would call me over put out his hand, and with a glint in his eye, say laughingly "How would you like to shake hands with a millionaire?" his great hand would envelop mine with a feeling of love, warmth, strength, and security.

That year Robert our youngest brother was born, Mrs Tustin asked if she could attend the birth, she wanted to experience the event. In those days fathers were kept well away, so I suppose it gave Mom some comfort. Up to now, she had given birth to three sons in very quick succession and often complained it was wearing her out. When asked by interested parties "Why have you had so many kids in the last few years?" She would answer "he comes home drunk, forces himself on me, and I get pregnant" She would then receive the expected sympathy and feel vindicated. This might have been a justifiable comment but that's how things were in those days.

Ross his third son born in 1955 and his fourth child, was to coin a phrase "the apple of his eye" Here I observed a very different side of dad. He warmed to Ross as I'd never seen him warm to anyone, possibly he observed in him a more kindred spirit to his own, the rest of his brood being too exuberant. When he entered a room and saw Ross his expression softened immediately. He would pick him up happily chatting away to him, take a seat putting the little fellow on his knee, and relax cuddling him. He looked the epitome of contentment and pleasure, a fulfilment realised. If only I'd had the time and opportunity to find out his feelings, I could have better understood his motivation. On my part, I hope there wasn't jealousy or resentfulness in any way, in fact, I believe my feelings were of being pleasantly and positively surprised. The rest of us were noisy, boisterous, and tiring, while Ross had a quieter, gentler disposition, more comparable to dads. Possibly we, Ross's siblings, inherited more excitable, noisy, extrovert genes more akin to Mom's disposition. Rather than the quieter, calmer, more diplomatic temperament Dad's personality exuded.

Robert was just a year old when Dad passed, so his interactions with him were probably negligible. In general, Dad treated Sonya, Scott, and me, evenly except for his violence toward me. In his time with us, I cannot remember him acting violently to anyone but Mom and me, I'm certain I would have remembered. Mom was often, very confrontational, and I was always in trouble and physical assault was a more accepted part of the culture in those days. This is not to say his actions were in any way excusable, but in the context of the times, they were not so unusual and not treated as criminal as they would be today.

Chapter 14 Farewell to Scotland

In 1957 as Easter approached, Dad suddenly declared he was going to visit his family in Scotland, and to my delight, he decided to take me with him. Whether it was for my benefit and to keep him company. Or possibly because Mo n m might have said you're not going, leaving me with all these kids. So, he took me to keep the peace, I can only conjecture, but I think the latter may have been the case. Robert was only a few weeks old so Mom must have been under severe pressure looking after the new baby, although Sonya was twelve and becoming more of a help, Mom still had a difficult time and a lot on her plate!

The date of our journey can be dated quite accurately because of two unusual events occurring while we were away. The first was the still unsolved murder of our local sweetshop owner on the 19th of April, and the second was a visit by the Queen to Oldbury just five days later. On her way there she went past our house; huge flagpoles were erected all along the route for her benefit. I did wonder why they had been put up in the first place but maybe due to security, it was kept a secret. They were soon taken down once she'd passed by. Such are the vagaries of life, for years nothing happens in our neighbourhood, then when we go away for a few days, a murder takes place, and the Queen visits us!

At the beginning of our journey, we first travelled through Wolverhampton, and to my surprise, they still ran trolley buses. They were powered by connecting great long forks on their roofs to overhead electrified steel cables, running high above the city streets., I'd never seen these before and at the time I was very impressed with them, sadly I never had the chance to ride in one; before they were discontinued in 1967. At the time, it was famously the largest trolly bus system in the world.

We gradually moved north, there were no motorways, so we used the old roads I can only guess the route and progress was slow. This wasn't helped by Dad's frequent stops, it almost seemed like he needed to refresh himself at every pub en-route. We stopped for a late lunch at a stylistic restaurant perched high on a hill overlooking a stretch of water possibly somewhere in Lancashire. It was very upmarket, and the lunch was very formal, I can remember ordering a pork chop, and when it arrived, complaining to Dad it was undercooked. He called the waiter over and berated him for the poor service and showed him the red blood still on the meat. How the situation was resolved I can only guess, but I have no further memories of the event.

Hanging around waiting for Dad as he supped a pint was second nature to me. Often, he bought me a soda pop to pacify my restlessness. It was at one of these locations that I first realised the geographical change in accents, overhearing a conversation about Dads' car, a woman speaking in a strange accent repeated his car registration number. Hearing this and to amuse myself while waiting, I recited it with the same vowel sounds and inclinations. Many years later I realised it must have been a Lancashire accent. At the time it gave me a rough idea of how to mimic a northern accent, and it helped me to never forget dad's car number.

Steadily moving north there appeared a large stretch of water to our left, the Solway Firth, and floating on its surface were several huge aeroplanes, dad told me they were Sunderland Flying Boats. He drove off the designated route to get a closer look and said with a nostalgic smile on his face "I've spent many a happy hour flying in them". Maybe if I'd been a little older, or more mature I would have asked him questions about this experience. It may have been that I did, and he didn't answer or I've forgotten his reply. Time has robbed me of further memories except that on other journeys and locations, we did come across these machines and Dad would stop; his face would lighten up, his eyes would water and there would be a long silence before moving on.

Before long we were crossing the border and entering Scotland, dads whole demeanour changed and he began springing up and down on his seat singing; "You Take The High Road And I'll Take The Low and I'll be In Scotland Before You" Soon we were passing through Gretna Green, famous at the time for young couples to elope to and get married by the Blacksmith, on the anvil at the Forge. In England, you would require the permission of your parents if you wanted to marry under the age of twenty-one. In Scotland marriage was allowed at sixteen without the need for consent, often newspapers would carry romantic stories of runaway couples escaping there to get married.

Towards late afternoon after travelling along country roads, we arrived at Rose Cottage in the county of Ayrshire. This was the home of Auntie Agnus Brown, it was a typical Scottish, country cottage on the grounds of a large dairy farm. Across the lane was a mirror image of Rose Cottage which was occupied by other family members, everyone seemed to be employed at the farm in some capacity.

Auntie Agnus Brown was what I imagined to be, a typical farmer's wife. She was tall, stout, with a large mop of grey hair surmounting a large round smiling face with apple cheeks. She wore a cross-over, finely patterned apron over her everyday clothes and a comfortable pair of plaid slippers edged with lambs' wool. We were welcomed into a sizable living room with a large rustic table in the centre, and along one of the walls stood a long narrow buffet table. This was a sight to behold, it was loaded with the widest range of baked items I'd ever seen. There were loaves of various types, buns and baps, scones, pies, and a multitude of delicious-looking cakes both large and small.

The room was packed and noisy, with mostly elderly and middle-aged family, chattering and laughing, what they were celebrating I'm not too certain but I think it was a birthday. Dad introduced me, and for a little while I was the centre of attention being the only Englishman there.

One man, an elderly person wearing a cloth cap and sporting a large grey moustache was introduced to me and coincidently we shared the same name. He hailed from Glasgow and appeared to be the party joker. He told me he would like to get to know me better, which made me feel important and very flattered. He asked me to put down my address so he could correspond with me and handed me a pencil and paper. The joke was, that it was a trick pencil, and when you tried to write with it nothing appeared. The whole room erupted with laughter, I felt very embarrassed and extremely disappointed. To my young mind, I felt cheated, this member of the family pretending to be interested in me. Encouraging me to believe I counted, when really, I was just bait for one of his jokes. Today, I would just see it as a childish prank of no importance and would laugh along with them.

Around the walls near the ceiling musical instruments were on display, and I was hoping someone would play them. Before I had time to become disappointed, Ian Innes a boy of about my age asked me to come outside and play football. He took me to a field ideal for a kick-around, it had a reasonably level surface and was surrounded by a high drystone wall with good quality well-mown grass. Soon several more boys joined in, and we had a good game, I was very impressed by their footballing skills, which I thought were much better than mine and the boys I played with back home. Later, because of limited space I was sent to the cottage on the other side of the lane to sleep, the people there were very welcoming. The bed that was allotted to me was full of boys all about my age.

One boy organised everyone else, showing me where to lay my head but before long, I was shaken awake. It was still dark, I looked at the clock it was only four o'clock, and the boy told me to get up and said "It's time for work" I followed the other boys to a milking parlour where the farmer gave us various duties. All the cows were Ayrshires, which have red and white markings and are slightly smaller than Friesians who have black and white markings and seem to dominate farming today. The milking facilities appeared very modern, lined with a combination of white-painted walls and ceilings with white glossy tiles. They were in two long lines of stalls for about a hundred cows with a wide aisle separating them. Milked by vacuum pumps, fitted into large shiny metal containers. Emanating from these were four rubber hoses with special ends that fitted the cow's teats, and the machine gently milked them. We had to empty the contents of these containers into milk churns and wheel them on a truck to the cooling shed. Here the milk was pumped out and over an all-metal, what looked like a washing board, but was a refrigerated cooling system. Today it is far more mechanised with hardly any human intervention, I believe the cows go into their milking booths and the process is computerised and fully automated. How much time we spent at the farm now escapes me, but I loved every minute and was very sad when Dad told me, we had to say our goodbyes and leave for Glasgow.

Who Auntie Agnus Brown was, remains a mystery, even after considerable investigative work using such search engines as "Ancestry" I remain thwarted. Dad referred to her in that way, so I assumed she was his aunt. The only one closely fitting that bill is the young sister of Dad's mother Isabella McCuaig, her name was Agnus McCuaig born around 1889 and she appears in the 1891 census aged two but disappears from all records after that. Her age would be about right, sixty-eight in 1957 and she may have married someone called Brown, but I can't verify it and Rose Cottage is one of the most popular house names in the UK. It was somewhere in Ayrshire, but I don't remember exactly its location so momentarily I'm stuck!

On the way to Glasgow, we popped in to see another relative, living in a small cottage nearby with his wife or partner. He was a wiry young man with black hair, dressed in vest and black trousers, they both gave us a happy and friendly welcome. We all sat down at a small table they smoked, caught up with the latest gossip, laughed, joked, and drank tea, I never found out who they were, possibly Dad didn't tell me.

The drive from Ayrshire was short and pleasant, as we approached the city you could see Glasgow's profile in the distance. Dad's reaction was one of elation, pointing out various landmarks with excitement, by his demeanour, you'd have thought it was New York. Mine was being underwhelmed and unenthusiastic which may have disappointed him. Leaving the farm and countryside may have affected my attitude and while Dad knew the agenda and was about to meet his close family, I was unaware of things to come.

It wasn't long before beautiful countryside began to give way to drab sandstone tenement blocks prevalent in the city then, and still common today. These were very imposing structures, made of sandstone, often several stories high, built right up to the roadside and running between road junctions usually hundreds of yards long, and are rarely seen outside Scotland. Many have now been replaced by concrete tower blocks and other more modern architectural designs. My eyes were then widened by the sight of great red rusty steel structures towering above us, we had reached the mighty river Clyde, here were its shipyards and the structures were ships in various stages of construction. Dad told me we were going to visit his brother Alec who lived nearby in Dumbarton Road which ran parallel to the river. He worked in the shipyards and was married to Mary, and they had two boys, one named John about my age, and Douglas a few years younger.

Their home was a block of flats, quite different from the usual tenements. Far more modern and conventional, the type of building you would see throughout the UK.

Only three stories high, the walls were pebble dashed and painted white with attractive balconies, breaking up what would have been an austere exterior. It is a sizable building containing many apartments, today its white exterior has been returned to the natural colours of the materials used, a pale brown. It blends in better now with its surroundings; and is not so dominating and overwhelming as the traditional Tenements. It is also surrounded by a small but pleasant fenced garden, mainly put down to lawn. This gives a softer more homely appearance, improving the quality of life for its residents.

We were welcomed warmly into their home, everyone was talking and laughing at the same time. Dad introduced me to the boys and his brother Uncle Alec and his wife Auntie Mary, he was slim and quite tall, the opposite of Dad. Auntie Mary was very much a woman of her time, with dark wavy hair in the style of the day, medium height, very attractive with a lovely smiling face. Neatly dressed in the everyday clothes of the working class, sporting the ubiquitous apron. She offered refreshments and quietly carried on with her housework hovering in the background supporting but not involving herself in the proceedings, the very opposite of the modern woman. As we settled in, I noticed Uncle Alec pick up a copy of the Topper comic, which I thought unusual, dad read books or newspapers but never comics. What I found remarkable was although he wore glasses, he still had to press his nose against the page to read. It reminded me of the comment made by my uncle Charlie who was an optician. He said, that because our grandma was born in Islay we had a defective eyesight gene, caused by inbreeding.

The living room was bare and poorly furnished as was all the rooms in the apartment. What he did in the shipyards I do not know but it must have provided a very limited income, his eyesight could have been a very restrictive factor in his career.

After lunch, except for Auntie Mary, we all headed over to Kelvin Hall a huge exhibition hall in Glasgow. It had on a Boy Scouts event and was possibly commemorating the fiftieth anniversary of the founding of the Boy Scouts movement. It was established by Baden Powell and that year there were special events, all over the world celebrating its founding. The hall was packed with people, and after a time I realised somehow, I'd become separated from Dad and the others. I searched the Hall for ages but, without any success. So, I decided to try and find my way back to the apartment. Which was over three miles away, in retrospect this was quite an ordeal for a young boy only aged eleven, in a strange city and not knowing the address. However, my sense of direction kicked in and I must have remembered several landmarks, one was a steel railway bridge with a distinctive crossband latticed framework, protecting the road it traversed. Also, a great help was the uniqueness of the building, a white smaller apartment block amongst those great monolithic tenements. When I arrived, the boys jumped up and down with excitement and wonder. They were amazed that I had made it back to their apartment, alone in a strange city. Dad just stood in the background and smiled, showing no signs of anxiousness at my disappearance, or relief at my return. My sister Sonya was researching family history between the late nineties and the new millennium and found the address of Douglas Innes one of Alec and Mary's sons. Speaking to him one of his first memories was about our visit in 1957, and how I managed to find their apartment after getting lost at Kelvin Hall.

That evening Auntie Mary served me my first-ever bowl of Scotch Broth, I asked, how was it cooked, and she told me it needed to be slow-cooked for twenty-four hours to tenderize the lamb and extract the best of its flavours. I was very impressed, and Dad's reaction was one of delight, pleased for my appreciation of Auntie Mary's efforts. The following morning, I was awakened by her lovely smiling face, happy and cheerful. Bringing in a hot cup of tea in one hand and the other my laundry, washed and ironed. She was to me the epitome of feminine care and loving kindness. In stark contrast to my treatment south of the border.

The boys then took me on a short walk around the area which I found rough and threatening. Children were playing in the streets, some with bare feet, shouting up to their mothers "Give us a piece of jam" in their strong Scottish accents, and from an open tenement window above, down it would come, to be deftly caught by some ragamuffin, I had never seen anything like this before.

On our return to the apartment, Dad said he was going to visit his brother James on the other side of the city. So, we left for the afternoon and drove across Glasgow to an even grimmer more rundown area. Dad parked the car outside a typical tenement block where his brother lived, I was surprised and disappointed when he made me stay in the car. He said, "Wait in the car, it's too rough for you in there, it's best you stay put" So I sat waiting bored and depressed by the Dickensian surroundings. After some time, I became aware that something was threatening my peace and security, so I turned my head to look behind me.

Right across Elderslie Street was a line of young men, dressed mainly in leather jackets forcing everyone to get out of their way. To avoid any kind of confrontation I slid gently down to the car floor, luckily this wave of potential violence passed by no one noticing my presence. Shortly after this incident, Dad returned, and as he began driving away started laughing, saying "You won't believe it but brother James was still in bed, hung over from the night before, one of his sons came in and asked for food, he pulled out a can of baked beans from under the bed and threw it at him" I cannot remember my reaction at the time but the thought of living like that still fills me with horror.

The following day was Sunday, and Dad and Uncle Alec decided on a trip to Loch Lomond, although the weather was overcast it remained dry. When we arrived, I was overwhelmed by its sheer beauty and was speechless at its contrast to the grimness of Southwest Glasgow, just a few miles away. The sky was lightly overcast but luckily the rain held off, the mood was joyful the men happily chatted away, and we boys exchanged anecdotes of our different life experiences. It was a happy day; we hired a rowing boat and went out across the loch visiting one of its tiny islands. It was quite magical, it had a small beach with a mixture of sand and pebbles, then just a few yards inland, towering lichen and moss-covered rocks surmounted with tall shadowy trees. It stirred your imagination. What if you were marooned and alone in such a place, how would you survive?

The return to Glasgow was short and uneventful, in the evening, after dinner Dad and Uncle Alec went out. On their return, a couple of hours later they brought a visitor with them, he was about dad's height wearing a cloth cap and a long gabardine raincoat. The three men stood in a line just inside the doorway, the stranger standing in the middle. He looked very similar to Dad and didn't appear that much older. He was introduced to me as my grandad! I was quite surprised by this revelation. Dad's recent illnesses had aged him significantly. Grandad took a step forward shaking my hand and, smiling took a half-crown from his pocket and gave it to me, Dad said jokingly "That's more than he ever gave me all my life" to which everyone laughed. It was a very special and memorable moment for me, we probably met when I was a baby living in Scotland, but I have no memory of that. Now I knew him and how he looked, walked, and talked. What I didn't know at the time was, it could have been the salient moment, when he handed Dad his share of the inheritance. It may have been pre-empted by Dad's poor health and the great possibility that he would outlive his son, which he did by two years.

Unfortunately, after the visit, and for many years, I lost all contact details of my Scottish relatives. So, in the early 1970s while holidaying in Scotland and visiting Kelvin Hall in Glasgow. My thoughts led me to wonder about Uncle Alec`s place, did he still live there? Would it be possible to retrace my steps, just like I did nearly twenty years before? Soon, I came across new viaducts, motorways, and new blocks of flats, it had changed so much, nothing seemed the same! So, I gave up the idea. Sadly thinking, I'll never be able to locate their apartment again. Then, in the new millennium, after another thirty years had passed, by chance I had some business in the center of Glasgow and was driving, this time from the west, the opposite side from Kelvin Hall. Three decades had passed, and no thoughts or intentions of trying to repeat my earlier, failed attempt, had entered my mind. Then, slowly like the gentle turning, of the volume knob on a radio, it started dawning on me, I was beginning to recognise my surroundings, I couldn't believe my luck.

Initially, I questioned my imagination, was my mind playing tricks? Then noticing what looked like Uncle Alec`s apartment block I stopped the car. It had been modernised and was no longer white, so I took a picture in the hope at some point it could be verified. A few years passed, but research, via Facebook and the Ancestry Database, eventually proved that by a lucky chance, I had found that very apartment over sixty years later.

The next day we were going home, we said our goodbyes, and then we began our long journey back to Birmingham, dad was quiet and a little sad he possibly had an inkling that he may never see his family or his Homeland again. He said we had one more visit to make before finally leaving Glasgow, it was to see May she was very ill in hospital with advanced Tuberculosis. He drove to a large cream-coloured clinic-type building, in the Art Deco style. Leaving me waiting in the car, outside the main gates. The weather mirrored the sombre feeling this unexpected diversion had put me in, Dad soon returned his mood even darker than before. He muttered she was very near the end, saying she had a plastic tube in her throat, I sat quietly. After a very long silence, he said smiling "Let's cheer ourselves up, take our time, and stop at any places of interest, such as castles and we'll have a look around" As we approached the border, he noticed a sign for Bruces Cave, and took a little detour to have a look, we observed a tall three-story square stone-built manor house in the Scottish architectural tradition. Its severe frontage was softened by a tower-like structure abutting its centre with a very long gothic-style window. Which must have given the inhabitants a much-needed relief and welcome illumination to their otherwise grim surroundings.

There were no other tourists about, so we had the place to ourselves, a tall, thin grey-haired old gentleman looking like the stereotype of an old "Antiquarian" did the honours. In the tower there were arms and armour of every description, he painstakingly described each item and how they were used. One item I remember vividly was a handheld spike-like item used for piercing chainmail. After which the old gentleman took us for a short, guided tour outside. Stopping at a cliff edge with wooden steps going down to a long platform, high above the river below. We walked along this till we reached the entrance of a man-made cave about twelve-foot square, quarried into the cliff face. It was all sandstone with crossbow slots cut into the stone, covering the entrance. In this cave, we were told Robert de Bruce hid, while on the run from the English. It was from here, the legend arose that from being broken and downhearted, he became revitalised and motivated. All, from watching a spider trying to weave its web and although failing many, many times, kept trying till it finally succeeded. Hence the saying "If at first you don't succeed try, try and try again" It may be just folklore, but he went on to lead Scotland to defeat the English at the battle of Bannockburn in 1314 which gave Scotland its independence.

The story of visiting the actual cave where Robert de Bruce watched the spider weave its web I have recounted as fact on many occasions. Only to find out recently, and with great disappointment, there are many caves in Scotland cited as the place where this legendary event occurred. It's no wonder Henry Ford said, "History is Bunk".

We soon continued our journey, returning to the main route home, The journey was uneventful and most of it lost over time, except for one traumatic incident. Still on the lookout for places of interest, I saw the word castle on some notice board, unfortunately, it was just the name of a golf course, and Dad had wasted time pulling over, which must have irritated him. Continuing to assume he wanted to meander back home taking in places of interest, I was sitting in the front passenger seat, excitedly looking all around for anything that might fit the bill. Suddenly he struck me very hard in the face, the irritation of the wasted stop and my head moving about in his peripheral vision must have caused him to snap. He said angrily "Stop looking at me" I felt I was just carrying out his wishes and was more upset than hurt, maybe the stroke had damaged his judgement and ability to cope.

Chapter15 Final Fling

We arrived home very late, early the following morning Dad called Sonya and me into the sitting room, he was dressed and ready to go off to work. He was sitting on the settee and next to him, rested a small leather case he'd brought back from Scotland. Smiling, he said "Look at this!" and opened the lid, our eyes must have come out on stalks! It was packed neatly with bank notes, we'd never seen so much money. Many years later, Sonya mentioned it must have been his father's gift of inheritance, given in advance, and the capital he used to build a new house.

Everyone was still talking excitedly about the two significant events that had happened while we had been away. The Queen's visit to Oldbury, which passed by our house, and the murder of a local sweetshop owner. Luckily, someone filmed the Queen's visit, and you can still see it on YouTube. The film was taken by an employee of Light Metal Forging Ltd a producer of aluminium alloy forgings for the aircraft industry. The film shows the front aspect of the factory, now sadly no longer in existence. Two of my uncles had worked there since the Second World War. Incidentally, much later my cousin and I also worked there. The two uncles were Bert and Bill Underhill, Bill received a letter after Her Majesty's visit from the Duke of Edinburgh, thanking him for the gifts of a Titanium Shooting Stick, for him, and a Titanium Rose Bowel, for the Queen. Uncle Bill's son Michael Underhill, now has that letter.

Whether Uncle Bert received a thank you letter, I don't know but there was some acrimony between them, I hope it wasn't the cause.

Then there was sadly, the mysterious murder of a local sweetshop owner, Fred Jeffs who I believe Dad knew, possibly because they were both Scottish and would have had a lot in common. You can also find details on that event if you look on YouTube, under the Stanley Road murder, sadly it's still unsolved. The only known witness was Fred's little dog. Dad showed me its picture in the paper, it was found wandering the streets and taken away in the back of a police van.

Whether Dad knew when he planned to visit Scotland or decided after, I cannot say but, on our return, he announced he was building a house. He then talked about getting the plans drawn up by an architect, and wanting a green roof although he worried about getting council approval for this unusual colour. One day in the early summer of 1957 he took me along to the building site, gave me a spade, and told me to start digging he also grabbed one and did likewise. After a short while, he said "That's enough, now at least we can always say we helped dig the foundations of our new house," it made me feel very important.

It is a lovely, detached property and when it was first built beautiful rolling green meadows could be enjoyed looking out from the large back garden. Unfortunately, a few years later the M5 Motorway and the Halesowen bye-pass were built through these meadows, detracting from the pleasurable vista. There may also have been a reduction in the length of the garden to facilitate the new roads.

It was centrally heated which was quite a luxury at the time, when dad said it was heated by oil, I imagined a pipeline running from a local garage, I had no idea about domestic oil storage tanks. Sonya had her own room being a girl, and like Mom and Dad's room, she would have a special strip light above her bed, she was very excited, and I was quite jealous. The fireplace and hearth were made of red brick, filled with white cement, in an arc-like design, reminiscent of the prewar period making an attractive and substantial central feature for the living room, which greatly impressed me.

He had quite a few run-ins with the builders and had to fire one group when he caught them idling. They had been dragging the job out for as long as possible, so becoming suspicious he visited the site without warning, catching them red-handed. It is always wise to obtain quotes for the completed job and build in penalties if they go over the time agreed, otherwise, they will inevitably take advantage and drag out the job for as long as possible. Dad may have been a bit too trusting in this regard, although his health was quickly deteriorating, and they may have thought they could take advantage of him. The house is in Alison Road, South Birmingham, in an area known to locals as Lapel.

We usually had the last week in June and the first week in July, for our fortnight's holiday, and 1957 was no exception. Dad had booked a cottage in Cornwall; it was in a place called Crackington Avon just a few miles south of Bude. It was a large, thatched cottage located on a farm, with a dirt road dividing the picturesque front garden from the working farm.

The living room window overlooked a beautiful meadow that ran down to a lively stream, on its opposite bank rose a steep hill on which grew thick woodland, filling the remaining view and climbing to a considerable height in the far distance. The sea was only about fifteen minutes' walk away but was hidden from the cottage by this hilly woodland, in the meadow below the cottage wandered saddle-backed pigs, geese, and ducks making an absorbing picture to a towny like myself.

On arrival, we were all standing on the threshold and about to enter the cottage when Dad turned around and faced us. Then, with a huge smile on his face and with great panache, removed his watch and announced, "On this holiday time will not be measured" Mom was not too pleased, the little ones were tired and restless and she said impatiently "Come on John let's get in and unpack."

Sonya and I looked sadly at one another and said nothing, even in our immaturity, deep down we knew time was running out and every moment was precious.

The weather that holiday was extremely good, I don't remember it raining, most days were sunny and hot. We became very friendly with another family who was also renting a nearby cottage, Mom and Dad socialising with them, Sonya and me playing with their son and daughter who were similar ages to us. Every day we would go off to the beach or borrow a boat and float up and down the stream. In Crackington Avon, there was just one shop which was mostly a post office. We took bottles back, to get the threepence deposit to help finance buying sweets and hiring surfboards, which compared to modern ones were very basic, but fun, nevertheless. We were warned by Dad not to wander without supervision onto the high headland, which was a significant feature of the place, recently a boy had fallen to his death climbing it. Which filled us both with fear and sadness for his family and their loss.

One morning, I found a dead seagull on the beach and thought it would be an ideal souvenir from our holiday, and taking it home would impress my friends and add to my kudos. So, I wrapped it in old newspapers and put it in a cupboard in the cottage. Dad found it, telling me in no uncertain terms, it was an idiotic idea, and threw it away. He should have made sure that I didn't know where he'd disposed of it because being a "little sod," I recovered my prize. Then took it back to the cottage and hid where it would be far more difficult to find. Soon to my amazement, the whole place was festooned with Airwick bottles, it looked like a green forest throughout the cottage. Airwick was the air freshener of the day; they were similar in size and shape to today's liquid soap dispensers but made of green glass. To make them work you removed the cap and pulled out a stout felt wick about as size of your middle finger, filling the air with a pleasant pine fresh odour. Dad must have spent a small fortune, but all to no avail. The cottage smelt disgusting, of fish, and rotting corpses mixed with the faintest odour of a pine forest. The farmer who owned the cottage was called in to investigate and spent several hours turning the cottage inside out, eventually finding my hiding place and the rotting carcass of the seagull, and to my chagrin, took it away. Although I fully expected severe retribution, surprisingly I was given the mildest of reproaches, maybe the continuing decline in Dad's health had modified his temper.

One morning Dad called me into the kitchen and showed me how to light a Primus stove and cook porridge, which has stood me in good stead over the years. However, he always used a pinch of salt which I have never done. He did it in such a warm loving and caring way, a side to him I rarely saw, believing this would have been more like his true self, had circumstances been different.

Halfway through our fortnight holiday, Dad decided to drive over to Paignton, possibly Mom persuaded him, so she could see her sister, our dear Auntie Flo. He hired a caravan in a lovely spot, just south of the town overlooking the sea at a place called Goodrington Sands. Sonya and I went down the harbour, the tide was out, and we found a couple of dead crabs. We brought them back to show Dad, he decided to boil them. A little later he said smiling, it was a waste of time, the seagulls had already taken all the meat. We were both disappointed, but a salutary lesson had been learnt, don't bother with dead crabs.

Dad possibly bored with Paighton took me on a trip crossing Dartmoor, with the usual visits to a few pubs on the way. He stopped a short distance away from its infamous and forbidding prison, giving me a brief history of it, which was interesting, and made a lasting impression on me. Hopefully, he was ensuring I never end up in there but there's still time! Alluding to drinking times, they were quite conservative in those days, and you could easily be left high and dry. Today they are much more liberal, and a serious drinker is under little pressure to find a watering hole to slake his or her thirst. Today, E.V. drivers must suffer from similar anxiety, as their batteries begin to run out of juice and charging points are too distant!

To solve this dilemma Dad had devised several strategies. Amongst these were, obviously knowing the times and places in your immediate location, being aware of the establishments that would stretch time restrictions, and those events that would be given special licences. The latter was an important backstop for thirsty situations, these could be sporting events, exhibitions, trade, and agricultural shows, etc.

By a very strange coincidence, on our trip across Dartmoor, we came across a local agricultural show, Dad parked up and he made his way to the beer tent while I wondered about its periphery, Dad disappeared inside to saviour its delights. The sun was shining, it was hot, and the surroundings fascinated me, cows, sheep, pigs, and horses after some considerable time Dad came out, slightly wobbly, and said it was time to leave. We made our way to the car and began our drive back to the caravan site. As we were crossing a narrow railway bridge, the car began to judder and make a terrible screeching sound. Unfortunately, the car had scraped the bridge wall, after traveling some distance Dad stopped and we both got out to inspect the damage. The wing was dented and there were innumerable, long white jagged lines, etched into the black paintwork. Dad cursed, and said, "Get back in the car" We returned to the car, and he drove off in a temper, only to be cut up by a milk float. He stopped the car and began berating the milkman. They both exchanged expletives, questioning whether their mothers had ever been married. We then drove on, a lesson in the futility of "road rage," which I should have learned all those years ago.

After the long weekend, the family returned to the Cornish cottage, one afternoon Dad decided on a trip to King Arther's castle in Tintagel. There is a group picture of this event, sadly Dad is looking old for his forty years, the stroke had made its mark, to the detriment of his appearance.

During the final week of our very last holiday together, we went for a day in Bude, it was very hot and sunny. Mom organised a comfortable spot on the beach and set up camp, Dad wandered off, and the hours ticked by. Mom began to complain, he was going to get food and he hadn't returned, she sent me off to look for him, I searched everywhere but couldn't find him. Getting hungrier I returned to Mom, who was still complaining but this time about him coming back with awful sandwiches, and he'd been drinking. They were cheese and tomato, wrapped in newspaper and had been lying around in the hot sun, the cheese was sweating, and the tomatoes were an almost inedible mush, worst still! he'd gone off again.

Sonya and I often talked about the mysterious woodland, that rose on the hills opposite, we wondered, if we climbed to the top, would you be able to view the sea? Also, what mysteries might be hidden amongst its tangled undergrowth? So, on the last day but one, we set off to explore. The trees were tightly packed and growing in between them was thick vegetation, of all the stinging and scratching varieties you can imagine. The nettles stung but worst were the masses of brambles tearing at my bare legs, in those days' boys wore short trousers giving little protection. Progress was very slow, and it was all too much for me, so I gave up. Sonya was more determined and carried on without me. When I returned, Dad asked me where my sister was, I told him I'd given up but she'd carried on through the woods and was trying to scale the hill. Dad was not too pleased, leaving my sister to fend for herself, and angrily told me so, in no uncertain terms. Sonya eventually returned giving up too, scratched and cut with great areas of nettle rash. Telling me what a wimp I'd been giving up so easily, and of course, she was right.

On our last evening, Dad said, "Come on Johnny, let's go for a walk" Eagerly I joined him, and we walked up the dangerous high point at Crackington Avon. When we reached the very top, he told me to get on my stomach and crawl slowly forward, he did likewise, and scaringly we crawled to the cliff edge. He then said smiling, and with an expression of sublime satisfaction "Look at that Sunset, you'll never see a better one" The sky was emblazoned with all the reds and golds imaginable, merging into the sea and sky with their myriad shades of iridescent ultramarine. The blood-red sun, slowly and remorselessly sinking below the horizon, was a beautiful reminder that all things must end. And Dad was right, I have never seen a better sunset!

The next day we were all in the car, packed- up ready to leave when Dad went back to the cottage for something. While we were waiting, Scott jumped onto the empty driver's seat and pulled the starter button, the car went bumping off along the road like a kangaroo on heat, scaring us all to death. Luckily Dad hadn't turned on the ignition, so the car came to an ignominious stop. After a few curses and complaints between Mom and Dad, we left Cornwall and returned home after our last and memorable holiday together, even little Robert experienced the event. He was just a few weeks old and spent most of his time in his carrycot.

Chapter 16 Compassion

Dad must have been extremely busy, with work, building the new house, and his health problems. Although the local pub allowed him to use their car park, whenever and for as long as he liked. He often parked his car on the roadside, opposite our house. One bright sunny day, I was looking out of the front bay window when careering down the road came a cyclist at breakneck speed. He was wearing a white cap and a yellow jersey, (he must have been a fan of the "Tour De France") his head was down, giving it all he had. I watched in horror as he crashed straight into the back of Dad's car!

His front wheel buckled against the bumper, his head hitting the boot with an almighty thump. The momentum forced him and the bike to rear up, passing the vertical position. Then fall back rapidly, sliding down onto the road, a tangled heap of arms and legs and distorted metal. A crowd gathered around the unconscious rider and his broken bike, I rushed out and joined the throng telling them "That's my dad's car!" The man started to come around, very dazed and confused, Dad came to the front door and called out "Bring him in here", so a couple of people helped him over to our house. He was a young man, in his late teens or early twenties, tall and very slim, he apologised for the damage. Dad said "That's of no importance don't worry about it" I had, expected fury and anger, after all, there was a huge dent and scratches to the back of his car. He was all kindness and care, I was amazed! he helped the guy and gave him a cup of tea, just before the ambulance arrived. Dad assured him his bicycle would be looked after, and he'd get it delivered to his home and forget all about the damage to his car.

On another occasion, Dad's car suddenly filled with smoke, and flames burst from the back seat, a bucket of water was thrown over it and Dad drove off unfazed by the incident. Then a few hours later the whole thing happened again much to everyone's amusement, except Dad's! This time he had to call the fire brigade to quench the blaze and thankfully they succeeded, but a new back seat and other remedial work had to be carried out to restore the upholstery. He told us a cigarette end thrown from another car must have gone through an open window, but nobody believed the story. It was suspected that he had probably dropped his cigarette without realising it. His deteriorating health possibly being a contributory factor.

Walking home one day, I noticed Dad's car parked outside with the lights on, it was dusk, so I thought no more of it. Sometime later he decided to go out, he disappeared to the car, only to return a few minutes later, cursing and swearing that the car had a flat battery. Innocently I chirped up "Oh yes Dad, I saw you'd left your lights on" Suddenly he gave me a mighty swipe round the head and said, "Why didn't you tell me earlier, you stupid bugger?"

He would often send me to the local shops for his favourite newspaper the Daily Express and his cigarettes; John Players and on occasions especially when he wanted to butter up Mom, a packet of Roses chocolates. They would weigh them out for you in those days, from a large, sweet jar usually in two or four-ounce lots, I always found tension mounting when they added or subtracted a sweet to balance the scales.

Another favourite of Dad was American crime fiction, there was a particular series of books that he liked with a yellow cover. He would send me to the local library to take back his old books and replenish his stocks.

One duty I performed regularly, at Mom's behest, was taking Dad's suits for repair. It was mainly the trousers and occasionally the jacket, suffering from unsightly cigarette burns. Whether it was because of his deteriorating health, or the drink these accidents happened, I wasn't sure. I never asked Mom and was never told but happily cycled along to the "Make-Do-and-Mend-Shop" on Waterloo Road, Cape Hill, Smethwick, to get them repaired. The little middle-aged lady who ran the shop was abrupt, very rushed, and business-like. Always with a cigarette dangling from the corner of her mouth, the ash momentarily defying the laws of gravity. She would carefully inspect the garment, her eyeglass lanyards giving her an air of intellectual superiority. Amazingly, she would quickly discover the area requiring repair, giving me a ticket with details of price, time, and date it could be collected. This I did and was always in awe of her skill at what was termed "invisible stitching" I thought it must be magic and she had some connection with the occult. Her terraced house was just opposite the shop, and in the window stood a manikin, displaying an embroidered pair of women's corsets which always made us boys' "Titter" with embarrassment.

Chapter 17 Nostalgia

With Dad`s approval, I joined Brandhall Scouts, and 1957 was a significant year in Scouting history. It was the fiftieth year of their founding and for this anniversary they were holding what was called "The Boy Scouts Jamboree" in August of that year. Boy scouts from all over the world assembled in the UK. The main encampment was at Sutton Park, north of Birmingham with satellite sites in surrounding parks. Our group, "Brandhall Scouts" were attending for one week, camping at Packington Park. Dad said I could go, giving me a cheque for the required ten shillings deposit. Embarrassingly, a week later I was called into the office at the scout hut and told by the very stern-looking scout leader, Mrs Wagstaff, and her accomplice that the cheque had bounced, and cash would now be required. Thankfully, Dad was not too angry when I told him, and he gave me a ten-shilling note instead. When I returned with the cash they seemed far more relaxed and jokingly her male assistant, said "Would you like to see how you can make ten shillings smaller without changing it" and rolled it tightly in the palm of his hand, after which he opened up the note and sure enough it was smaller, I was surprised that such an important person could make such a stupid joke and walked away in disdain.

Leaving for camp Dad allowed me to use his old R.A.F. kit bag which was white with a broad blue band around its middle made of stiff canvas It was like a big round sack, open at one end with large brass eyelets threaded with a drawstring to secure its contents.

He also gave me a one pound note, for spending money. This was extremely generous for the time and is over thirty pounds in today's money, my fellow scouts had only a fraction of this, I was showing off with great exuberance, boasting how well off I was. When it suddenly disappeared, we searched high and low, asked all around, and went to lost property all to no avail. So, from being possibly the most well-off scout, I went completely broke. All that week I had to watch my friends buying ice creams, sweets, and other goodies while I had nothing, it was a very long week. On reflection, it was probably stolen by a trusted friend. I never told Dad, I was too ashamed for treating his beneficence so badly, when he asked how things went, I told him I'd had a great time.

We had one very enjoyable outing at the end of summer, Mom wanted to visit her sister, Auntie Flo. She was four years older, and bossed Mom in that big sister way. She was a tough, old bird with a great sense of humour, who for various reasons hadn't had the easiest of lives. Auntie Flo had made a bigger effort, than Mom, to escape her Black Country roots. Speaking in what you might say a sort of "Received English" accent that would disappear in confrontational situations. At the time, she was living at an RAF station where she was the catering manager. It was near High Wycombe which is a prosperous town on the River Thames about fifty miles from London. It was just an overnight stay, the accommodation was utilitarian, very basic, single-story units built during the war. I suppose you might call them huts; Auntie had made hers comfortable and homely.

The adults were drinking and reminiscing, laughing and joking so I sat by a small bookcase and read haphazardly through her collection. They were mostly books for grownups, not remotely interesting to me, then I spotted an old Victorian medical book, the pages were yellowing with age, but it had illustrations that amused me. The one I remember most clearly was "The Tape Worm" Its drawings and descriptions put me in fear for my life, franticly checking to make sure I had none of its symptoms.

Possibly the most vivid memory of the visit, was at breakfast the next morning. It was a bright sunny start to the day. Dad was distracted from his coffee and toast by the sound of chattering and laughter, he moved to the window to find out its cause. Walking along the tarmac road were a group of about a dozen young men, in blue trousers and light blue open-necked shirts with white towels slung over their shoulders, obviously enjoying their camaraderie and the warm sunshine. "They must be off to the showers," he said half smiling in a muted voice. Possibly, his past came flooding back evoking a longing for his days in the Air Force.

After breakfast, we packed up all our things, including some pilfered R.A.F. goodies by way of the beneficence of Auntie

Flo, loads of biscuits, and most memorable a catering-size tin of Nescafe instant coffee. Then we climbed into the car and waved our goodbyes to Auntie Flo but instead of going straight back home, Dad said "We're going to Windsor Castle". I don't know why he wanted to go there but we all got excited about visiting this famous place, and even Mom didn't complain.

We toured the castle and a very friendly Japanese man, and his wife came up to me and started to ask questions about my life in the UK. He looked very neat, wearing a dark blue blazer, brown trilby hat, and steel-rimmed glasses, he kept bowing his head to every question I answered, his camera almost hitting me in the face. Dad came over and politely interjected, steering us discreetly away.

What impressed me most was the man's camera, I'd only seen the "Kodak, Brownie Box Camera," this was entirely on another level. Mainly silver, with a massive lens and lots of complicated dials, I coveted it but knew it was way out of my league. The war had not been over that long and meeting someone from Japan made me feel very uneasy, I think Dad felt the same. Later we purchased a few souvenirs from the gift shop mainly sew-on badges and a sword and shield for me, and then made our way back home.

Chapter 18 A Bitter Blow

Towards the end of 1957, Dad became sadder and quieter than his usual self. He was that way inclined anyway, so possibly only those very close noticed the subtle difference. He started going occasionally to the local Baptist Church, he had always kept any religious thoughts to himself, so this was quite a revelation. However, in the past, he had mentioned, that when he was young, he had regularly attended Sunday school. His bible knowledge was quite extensive, I remember him telling me that back in his youth in Glasgow, he had been awarded certificates for it.

Doctors continued to warn him that his lifestyle habits were destroying him, unfortunately, he was passed all that and was living for the moment. The new house was steadily progressing and would soon be completed. His brother Jim who would be driving through the area would now and again drop in, sleeping on the settee. His Glasgow accent was almost incomprehensible to me, dad naturally had no problem understanding him. He always looked unkempt, unshaven, and smelt of body odour, but he was always welcomed and looked after.

Hogmanay was approaching and for the last few years, Dad had made a special effort to celebrate it. He invited friends, and Sonya and I were allowed to stay up, dad played his LP of Jimmy Shand and his band singing all the Scottish favourites over and over again. They were very memorable and enjoyable moments.

All that came to an end on the 17th of March 1958. On my return from school, Mom was very flustered, she asked me to go to Smethwick and get some mince for Dad's tea, it was one of his favourites. She was so firm about this, that I had to agree, riding my bike on about a seven-mile round trip.

It seemed well "over the top" even for Mom and I had to do it before Dad arrived home. All this effort and Broadhurst & Son, the local butchers were only a short walk away, I can only suggest that she must have run out of money. Therefore, sent me to Marsh & Baxter's in Smethwick who would always supply her with meat "On tick." Mom always had a very good rapport with the retailers on the High Street. On arriving back, I went straight to the kitchen, unaware that Dad had already arrived home, from work. Standing with my back to the room, unwrapping the parcel of mincemeat on the countertop. He rushed by me and said, "See you later Johnny I'm off out" Surprised, I turned round and said, Okay Dad," I can picture him now his dark fawn gabardine mack swirling with the turn of his body as he quickly opened the back door and was gone, out of my life forever.

That evening all seemed as usual, I'd gone to bed and was fast asleep, when I was immediately awakened by a loud knocking on the front door. This was very unusual for two reasons, first, it was very late, around midnight, and secondly, when I went to sleep it was almost impossible to wake me. A few weeks earlier, everyone had gone out, leaving me in charge of the house, all the doors were locked, and every window shut. They banged on the doors and rattled the windows all to no avail, in the end, Dad had to smash a window to get in. He was not very happy and gave me a good telling-off. I didn't feel guilty, after all, you can't help sleeping too deeply.

However, this time, the loud knocking on the front door instantly woke me, I was wide awake and fully alert. I heard Mom muttering something under her breath as she shuffled to the front door saying loudly "Is that you John?" before she opened it a man's voice said "No it's the police" The door opened.

The man spoke again and said "Mrs. Innes, wife of Mr. John Innes" Mom replied in a weak and frightened voice, "Oh it's a policeman, yes, what is it?" Sympathetically he said "I'm sorry to tell you but your husband is dead" She screamed "Oh no, oh no, it can't be" repeatedly, over and over again, it was heart-wrenching.

Immediately I went straight into Sonya's room. She was worn out and fast asleep. Having returned late from the Princess Hall Picture House, she had seen the Elvis Presley film "Jailhouse Rock" which she had been raving about. Still in shock, I shook her awake and simply said "Dad's dead" How we made it through the night I don't know, but I remember wandering around the house the following morning. Looking at all his things, toothbrush, razor, an unopened packet of Tootle ties, shoes, clothes draped over a chair, etc. In the tearful realization that he will never need them again, envious of my brothers, whose innocence and age protected them from the catastrophe that was unfolding before us. Their resilience would get them through in the short term, but such a loss always has long-term consequences that are almost undefinable.

Mom told me later, after I'd gone to bed, he came home complaining about having stomach pains. It was very late in the evening and the shops were shut, so he was going to Boots. They offered an all-night chemist service in Birmingham, which was about a twenty-minute drive away, here he would be able to get something to ease the pain. He was walking to the Perryhill Tavern, where he parked his car, it was just a few hundred yards away, but he never made it. Collapsing onto the pavement about halfway, and dying of a heart attack, he was found by the local policeman, but unfortunately too late.

That one traumatic moment taught me a very helpful lesson, but much too early in life. When you lose someone of that magnitude, the world you knew has gone forever. To come to terms with that realisation, you must go through the "process of grieving" a complex but undeniable one, it's necessary for your survival. Everything, that you knew was for certain, is broken into little pieces, your old world has gone forever, never to be, again. You need to build a new one from the bits left over, but it can take years. His postmortem revealed he had died from a coronary thrombosis, Mom told us that the doctor said, "his heart was like that of an old man's, and the stroke had been far more severe than first thought." Due to his sudden death and being found outside, late at night, the police became temporarily involved. Mom was questioned and asked particularly about what he had eaten that day. A forensic team tested food samples from the kitchen cupboards and searched around the house and his car but soon thankfully gave the all-clear.

It was a crippling blow to the family, regrettably, we never moved into the new house he'd built for us. Mom sold it, with his car and all other things belonging to him. His whole estate of five thousand pounds went to her which would be worth just over one hundred and fifty thousand pounds in today's money. If she had kept the house, it would have been worth over half a million pounds today, which demonstrates how high house inflation has been in comparison to other necessities.

At the time, selling the new house was possibly the right decision after all the council house we lived in was in good condition and comfortable. The money gave her an excellent cushion against economic difficulties and together with her other income provided the family with a reasonable standard of living.

There are few photographs left of him, sadly I have just one, a poor and damaged one taken at a wedding reception, blown – up from a large group photograph taken in 1954. In my memory only, there was one of him with a group of boys, looking like street urchins when he was about ten years old, one in his twenties riding a horse looking very happy, and that special studio portrait in his RAF uniform.

Dad was buried in Quinton cemetery I am not sure who attended, but I'm certain his brothers Alec and James came from Glasgow for the funeral, and Cousin Robert now residing in the USA, was a Pallbearer. Mom never visited the grave after that day. When asked why, she would become very defensive and say "I believe, you do your best for them when they're alive, there's no point being false and doing things after they've gone" which I suppose is fair enough, I don't remember her visiting anybody else's grave either. Unfortunately, she held a considerable amount of bitterness towards Dad. We his children asked her over the years if we could mark his grave, but such was her attitude towards him, it was not allowed. So, it wasn't till after her death in 2006, that we were able to finally erect a headstone to his memory.

Conclusion

Apart from my memories, all I have left of Dad is the RAF certificate of service and discharge. How it survived all these years is nothing short of miraculous and I wouldn't have that but for the kindness of my brother Ross, who gave it to me a few years ago.

It was a paradoxical experience attempting to piece together my knowledge, experience, and memories of Dad. Trying to be as truthful as possible knowing that memory can play tricks on you, and what you think is fact can be fiction and vice versa, or even a mixture of both. All I can say I've done my best to communicate to the reader the man who for better or worse was my dad.

It is from my perspective, but a modern version of dad would be my son, Ross, his genetic mix may be much closer than mine. He is a similar build and looks very much like him and what's more important they are or were both happy to work quietly without fuss or bother, getting the job done. The extreme extrovert characteristics, probably, inherited from my mother, don't appear to have been passed on. Giving Ross a quieter more studious disposition, reminiscent of Dad.

Mom often said of him "he liked to keep himself to himself" which might have been true to some extent, but he also liked to spend a lot of his time "in the pub" which is a very social setting. Uncle Charlie an optician by profession, a warm and generous man, who knew Dad well, talked about him in detail one day.

It was in the early eighties; Someone told me he was seriously unwell, so I paid a visit to his home. Auntie Doll, his wife took me to the "Sun House" at the bottom of their garden, on the way she told me, very bravely, he had the onset of Dementia. Uncle Charlie was sitting in a comfortable chair, and although it was mid-afternoon, he was still dressed in his pyjamas and dressing gown, he looked very relaxed and was happily puffing away on his pipe. He welcomed me in his usual warm and friendly way, gesturing me to sit down next to him. We sat and talked; he asked me questions about Twigworth Rectory a property that was up for sale, and I'd been recently viewing. He also asked other personal questions, so everything seemed as usual. Then he began to talk about his investments and showed me papers with financial details together with company listings. This was very unusual, such information he would never normally share with me. So, I became aware that his normal reticence had declined. We drank tea and he offered me a fill of my pipe which I gladly accepted, and we both puffed on our pipes chattering happily away. Suddenly out of the blue, he said, "Your dad was a Gentleman!" he then went on to say; "he was a lovely man, kind, generous, quiet, friendly, and highly intelligent," he hadn't a bad word to say about him. Then he started to talk about Mom and said almost the opposite about her. It saddened me greatly to hear this unabridged account of her, and her attitudes and personality, but I couldn't argue, it was what I knew, from other sources and my own experiences.

As I was taking my leave, Auntie Doll took me to one side and whispered. "Do you remember halfway through your visit, his favourite Sister Eadie, popped in to say goodbye to him?" I replied, "Yes of course," worried, she could be thinking I had dementia too. "Well, you watch this," she said. Taking me gently by the arm and leading me back to Uncle Charlie. He was still sitting there happily puffing away on his pipe. "Charlie, did you know your sister Eadie has been for a visit and has now gone home?" she asked, softly. "Oh No I've missed her" he sadly replied, with a look of annoyance on his face. She then went on to tell me his sister had spent at least an hour with him chatting away, just before I had arrived. "And now he has no memory of her visit, and when you leave, he will have no memory of your visit too, It's breaking my heart" she sobbed, tears running down her troubled cheeks. I gave her a hug and a kiss on the cheek and left, with a feeling of great sadness. Realising my powerlessness, at being able to make any useful contribution to the events, that would naturally unfold, as the disease progressed, if that's the right word.

There were, as far as I know, never any photographs of Mom and Dad's marriage, which is strange. The war presented great difficulties and shortages, money would have been very short too, but most people had at least one photograph of their special day.

It was not a good omen, for a successful outcome. It has been said that opposites attract and that may have been the case in their relationship. But in the long term, it was possibly not the best formula for marital bliss. They were married in the January of 1944 in Smethwick, it's on record so there is no doubt about it.

Dad was twenty-seven when he married Mom and she was twenty-one, he would have been quite worldly, and mother possibly a little naïve. He had been in the RAF for seven years at the time of their marriage and served a total of twelve years. It was an institutionalised environment; very structured and predictable he would have had established comrades and although some of his postings were short, he would have had to adapt to his new surroundings quickly. All his needs were provided for; food, clothes, hygiene, and billeting without requiring any input. His work would have been scheduled, predictable, and guaranteed. He had a quiet, thoughtful disposition and was quite intelligent, the RAF prewar entrance requirements were quite stringent. In his educational years, Scotland had some of the best schools anywhere, so the quality and standard of his education would have been high. He was mainly an introverted personality type, happy to go unnoticed, steadily working away at any task necessary to get the job done. A team player, willing to give and take orders without any fuss. He was a mild-mannered man with an underlying Christian belief system.

In Scotland the women in his life, his mother, sisters, and aunts still interacted with their menfolk in the old-fashioned way. Emancipation was changing women's roles and position in society, and this may have been progressing quicker in the South.

The war accelerated these changes, women were doing many of men's jobs and weren't prepared to return to being just housewives, they wanted their careers and say in post-war society. The Scottish women I observed were gentle, quiet, supportive, warm, and loving. They were the traditional women, housewives, and mothers. The builder of the home environment, quietly going about the business of feeding the family, caring for the children making sure her man was fit and well. Able to go out and earn their daily crust. I'm not giving any opinion on the rights and wrongs of this it's just how I observed the situation at that time. Things have changed considerably today and so have attitudes for better or worse, it's not for me to judge.

His expectations of married life in England may have been far from its reality, our mother's naturally outgoing personality, inherent anger, speed of taking offence, and unjustifiable persecution complex would have been difficult for anyone to interact with. She also could not project warmth in the maternal, natural way. She was possibly more a product of her time, caught up in the old ideas of what a woman's role was in society. All the restrictions and limitations, and now the progressive world of equality. She was quite intelligent and had to wrestle with these thoughts and with the old ideals of being subservient, and in the supportive role, she was brought up to understand. This could have tormented her and many others in her generation. Having a bright mind, she may have perceived what could have been, but for her sex and class. This realisation can be a bitter pill for anyone to swallow.

Dad may not have realised, how effective living with his in-laws was at keeping his marriage reasonably settled and calm. That was, until he attempted to relocate to Glasgow. In the short time we were there, he probably encountered a portent of how future married life was likely to unfold. Therefore, to calm things down we swiftly returned to Smethwick. Although, the official reason for our return was to find work!

When we first moved to our new house in 1954 Dad was slim, fit, and seemed to cope with life reasonably well. The rapidness of his decline was breathtaking, drink played a significant part in this, together with his matrimonial difficulties. A prevalent drinking culture existed in both Glasgow and the RAF, one of Mom's rare comments about living there was his brothers often got so drunk they fell asleep and peed themselves.

Also, today we have an improved understanding of the mental health problems suffered, after leaving active service in the armed forces. It is called Post Traumatic Stress Disorder (PTSD.) There was very little help, or no help at all, for this syndrome in Dad's time. Thankfully, these days we have a better insight into this problem, and more aid can be given. Trying to navigate through civilian life can be overwhelming for ex-servicemen and women. His job in Buying; further exacerbated the situation. Every day he received bottles of free whiskey and cigarettes from his suppliers, adding to his difficulties in trying to resist temptation. Therefore, as his consumption of both increased, his health inevitably declined.

His violence towards Mom and me may have been driven by a complex amalgam of drink, marriage, and civilian life. Also, violence to women and children was far more acceptable and to some extent expected in his generation, added to alcoholism it can become significantly more virulent and dangerous.

Mom and Dad were possibly not suited to being married and raising a family. Things could have been very different if they had met people more suited to their personalities; and had the good fortune to marry more compatible partners.

It may be wishful thinking, or to bolster my ego but I've always felt that Dad had a sort of a "Guardian Angel" influence on my life. It's difficult to accept, that an important person in your formative years will suddenly disappear from your life, forever.

Certain events may have been just coincidental but have left me thinking, was he there gently guiding me? The chain of events leading up to me unintentionally being in the same profession. The RAF guy I chatted to just after my sister's passing. These are just some things that have made me wonder, one incident above all gave a very powerful sign of divine intervention. Crashing my motorcycle on a very difficult bend, just after heavy rainfall. Skidding with the machine and being thrown against a concrete lamppost, the both of us ending up in the middle of the road. My face down upon the tarmac and feeling paralysed, thinking I've done it now, my backs broken. Then losing consciousness and coming around, sometime later, realising I was surrounded by police and ambulance men. Quickly jumping up and asking "Where's my motorbike?" and being told it's been taken away and to get in the ambulance. Although I tried to decline their invitation, they all insisted even though I pleaded with them "But there's nothing wrong with me" At the hospital, I was given a full medical examination, and no injuries were found, whatsoever! Despite my helmet and leather jacket being badly damaged, not even a bruise was found, it seemed impossible. The only conceivable explanation, after considerable bewilderment was that dad was looking out for me. There are many other situations in my life where his support or guidance appeared to influence the outcome, inexplicable and some unbelievable.

To conclude, he was born into a working-class family. To parents who believed in contributing to society within the scope of their allotted positions. His father was a Baker all his working life, and his mother was a domestic servant before her marriage. They always lived in rented accommodation, mainly tenements in Glasgow. His environment would have been very grim, surrounded by shipbuilding and heavy engineering. These were the main sources of employment in the Govan area of Glasgow. His father was a Baker and so was one of his brothers, so he may have been more optimistic than his friends about future career opportunities. He was intelligent enough to realise joining the RAF would improve the quality of his life and clever enough to find a supporting role for himself in the service. Whether drinking developed in his early civilian days, or the RAF is not recorded but the culture was prevalent in both spheres of his life. Using it possibly as a social stimulant in the beginning and an escape when trapped in later years. He would have known the consequences of his addiction and maybe he saw no alternative. He was quiet and undemonstrative by nature, a natural introvert, modest and kind. He was a good man much loved and much missed by me, while writing this I felt his presence and hand on my shoulder. He still enters my dreams after all these years, in different scenarios but always the same theme! "The parable of the Prodigal Son" but with our roles reversed.

THE END

Printed in Great Britain
by Amazon